50 Shades of Money

Debbi King

Printed in the United States
ISBN 978-0-692-05593-9

Published by Lovell Press

Table of Contents

Introduction

Have you ever been dealing with something in the area of your money and wished you could get advice on what your options are and what is the best way to handle something. Well, wish no more.

I decided to write this book because in all my years of coaching, speaking and writing, I noticed a trend – I noticed the same questions being asked over and over. Maybe some of the numbers were different and the names were changed, but the core of the questions were the same. This told me that there is a need for this information and since my only goal is to serve you the best way I can, I wrote this simple, easy to read book just for you!

My first book – the best selling, award winning "The ABC's of Personal Finance" – covers everything I learned on my journey from being a single mom making $10,000 a year and having over $200,000 in debt to reaching financial freedom. It covers not only the math, but the emotional side of money as well since personal finance is 10% math and 90% emotions. And then my second book – "26 Weeks to Wealth and Financial Freedom" – is a 26 week plan to set you up for wealth and financial freedom.

This book, however, is practical. It answers the top fifty questions that I get asked on a daily basis and answers them in as much detail as I can. Whether you have just decided that you want to begin the journey to wealth and financial freedom, or you have been on the journey for quite some time, this book is going to give you good, practical advice from someone who has been in the valley and has risen to the mountaintop.

I would like to caution you however. Just like anything else, nothing will change without action. You can read this book, my other books, blogs or anyone else's material and nothing will change without action. Having the information is not enough – it must come with follow through. Unfortunately, I can't do this for you. I wish I could because I want nothing more than the best for you in all areas of life but especially in your finances.

We were not made to struggle. We were designed to be happy and enjoy life. But along the way, many times, we let our emotions get the best of us and we make unwise decisions. This can cause us to have stress in our lives. But there is hope. I am a living example of this hope. I didn't receive a magic wand or win the lottery to get rid of my debt. I worked hard, made better decisions and developed a lifestyle of good decisions that have sustained me through the last 15 years.

Know this – you may have made bad decisions in the past. Maybe you are like I was and it seems like every decision you make doesn't work out. Today is a new day! You get to start over, fix the past and have an awesome future. And I am going to help you anyway I can. Let's start with this awesome book.

Today is a clean page. You are the author of your story. Write a best seller!

Most Asked Question

I wanted to start with the most asked question that I receive – I am asked this multiple times a day and my answer never changes no matter how many "buts" you add to it. And I think by the end of this chapter, you will agree with me.

"My child is going off to college and they 'need' student loans in order to pay for it. Should we cosign for them or get parent loans in our names?"

Later on in this book I will address the issue of paying for college and student loans at which point you will understand why I put the word "need" in quotes. But right now I simply want to address the issue of cosigning.

I do not care if it is for a student loan, an apartment rental, a credit card, a mortgage or any other possible thing someone might need a cosigner for – the answer to this question is always no! I don't care if it is your child, your parent, your aunt or an acquaintance – the answer is always no!

Now don't misunderstand me – I am not a heartless person who doesn't understand the "needs" of others. I am someone who has had a relationship ruined because someone cosigned for me and I learned from that experience what I am about to share with you. Also, as a person of faith, I believe that there is a reason God states multiple times in the Bible to never cosign for another.

First of all, when a person needs a cosigner it is because they cannot get what they want on their own. Either they have no credit, bad credit, not enough income, or are too young to have a solid credit history. All of these should be loud warning bells going off in your gut warning you that this is a bad idea. We all get this warning, but many times we ignore it because it is our child or parent or someone we care deeply about that is asking. One time, our son came to us and asked his dad and I to cosign on an apartment with him. At that point, we had already learned the lesson I am teaching you the hard way. Therefore, we made the very hard decision to tell him no. However, we did offer to help him find a place even give him a little money if needed, but we couldn't put our name on his lease. He was disappointed and probably a little angry (scared is more likely the feeling he had), but within a few weeks, he had found a place in his budget that would rent to him without a cosigner.

In our example, we knew that our son had every intention of paying his rent every month and pay it on time. But having lived life a little bit, we also knew that intentions weren't always reality. I believe that very few people would ask for your help with the intention of not paying – they intend to pay. But what happens if they can't (and to this point they don't have a great track record or they wouldn't need a cosigner).

What happens when they can't or won't pay or they pay late is your credit takes a hit. When you cosign you are not simply saying "this person is okay" – you are betting your financial reputation on it – literally. You are just as responsible as they are if they miss a payment or are late.

Never put your financial reputation (credit) or your financial future on the line for someone else including your kids. I know firsthand this is hard and nowadays it seems like parents hardly ever say no to their kids. But when it comes to cosigning it is a must. Look for other ways to help them – like we did – or give them a little something as long as it doesn't enable the problem, but never give them your signature.

And to answer the direct question at the beginning of the chapter – do not cosign for your child when it comes to student loans. Education is not an exception to the answer of no! There are no exceptions to this answer. Skip ahead to page 129 to find out about paying for college and how to do it without ruining your finances. And as for a parent loan, this should be a last resort and only for the amount that you can pay off in 2 years without disrupting your finances. You are looking ahead to retirement and you need to keep your focus on you. That sounds selfish I know, but if you go into debt to put your kid through college, who is going to support you when you retire? It won't be your kid. You must find a balance between helping if you can without endangering your financial future. In many cases, this means not putting anything towards your kid's college and that is okay.

Life is not a popularity contest. You can't make financial decisions based on people liking you and you not disappointing them. People have expectations of us and when we don't comply, they get angry. However, their expectations cannot be what guides our decisions. Personal finance is personal – meaning you need to do what works for you and you alone. No one else is living your life or walking in your shoes. Live your authentic life – not anyone else's!

Most Asked Question – Part 2

"My mother keeps asking me and my siblings to loan her money. She doesn't have a budget, spends money all the time and then comes to one of us when she doesn't have enough to pay her bills. Should we keep loaning her money since she is our mother and if not, how do we stop the cycle?"

This is the second most asked question that I get. It is amazing how it is not "how to get out of debt" or "how to start saving" – it is about supporting people who should be supporting themselves.

Just like cosigning, it is never okay to loan a friend or family member money – no exceptions. This will never end well. Even if they pay you back, there will always be an unspoken tension there. Even if they make all the payments agreed upon on time, there will always be a judgement of every purchase they make from now on. The question above is an extreme one that we will address – it has deeper issues than just loaning someone money. However, no matter what the circumstance, it is never advisable to loan someone money.

Now, having said that, if you have a situation where someone truly needs your help, for example a job loss, and they are doing everything they can to make ends meet and you want to help them out once, do so with a gift – without an expectation of repayment. There are two questions to ask yourself before handing over the gift – am I enabling bad behavior and can I afford to give this money? You never want to enable someone to continue to make bad decisions and you must not ever put yourself in financial peril to help someone. This is one of the awesome advantages to reaching financial freedom – it gives you the ability to help someone who is truly in need.

Now to address the specific question – it is extremely possible that you are in a similar situation with a friend or family member or it may be possible that you are the person always needing help. That's okay – either way we are going to end the cycle today.

I had this same problem for many years of my life. I was the person always in need and my parents were my crutch. Every time I needed a car or had an emergency, I was always turning to them knowing that they would say yes. One day, many years later, they actually said no. It was the worst and best day of my life. It was the worst day because I didn't have a way to deal with my problem. I wasn't prepared for an emergency and my parents were my emergency fund. I didn't have a budget of any kind and I had the mindset of buy now and figure out how to pay for it later – a horrible plan by the way.

The day my parents told me no was also the best day of my life even though I couldn't see it then. It was the knock on the head that I needed to get my act together. You see, as long as I had a crutch, I would never walk on my own. I did end up having to file bankruptcy and start over, but that journey made me research and learn all I could about the proper way to handle money and carried me all the way through to the financial freedom that I have today.

I know that it was extremely hard for my parents to finally tell me no. Just like it was extremely hard for this young lady and her siblings to tell their mother no. Of course, the mother got angry and wouldn't speak to them for a while, but that anger stemmed from the fear of losing her crutch. By telling her no, they gave her no other choice but to find another way to pay her bills. We worked with her to establish a budget, we helped her get to the root of her money issues and we taught her how to make better decisions – decisions that would move her forward instead of backwards. As we discussed with cosigning, when you tell someone no, they aren't going to be happy. But you need to make decisions that are best for you and in the long run best for them. Offer to help where you can – buy a book, help them set up a budget, help them with ideas on how to raise the money. And if they refuse that kind of help, they aren't ready to change. They were probably using you as their personal ATM.

Many people want help when they hit bottom, like our mom in our example. But there are many who simply want someone else to do it for them. Either way, by saying no, you are helping them whether they see it or not. And let me say one last thing – it took me many years before I realized that my parents telling me no was the best thing they could have ever done for me and I thank God every day that they did. Just say no!

Budgeting – Regular and Irregular

Your money is going to go where you tell it – whether you know it or not. When you run out of money at the end of the month it is not because you weren't paid correctly and it wasn't because the bank took it. It is because you made decisions with your money throughout the month and it went exactly where you told it to go. However, if you are telling your money where to go without a road map or a plan, you are going to get off course and you have no one to blame but yourself.

"I don't feel like I need a budget. All I ever hear about from financial blogs is budget, budget, budget. But I get along fine without one. I am able to pay my bills and make ends meet without an official budget. Why is this term so popular and why does everyone say it is a must?"

People hate the word budget. As soon as you say it, people will tune you out. If I gave a seminar on budgeting, no one would show up. However, if I give one on wealth building they sell out. But guess what the number one thing millionaires say is the key to building wealth. You guessed it – budgeting.

Look, I get it. Budgeting can be challenging if you are not a numbers person and many people believe that they have a budget because they have limits in their heads. People also believe that budgets are limiting and take away the freedom we want to enjoy when it comes to our money. I actually don't use the word budgeting. I believe that what you really need is a spending plan. You would never build a house without a blueprint or some sort of plan. And the same goes for your finances. You will build the best house when you have the best plans and you will build more wealth when you have specific plans for your money.

Budgets or spending plans as I will call them are not evil. They are not designed to tell you what you can't do. They are designed to help you see what you can do and live within your means and help you reach your goals and dreams. For example, everyone advises, including God, that you save 10% of your income for the future. If you do this your entire life, you will have enough to get you through when the time comes that you decide to not work anymore or start something new in the next chapter of your life. Just 10%. Everyone can do this. But most people think they can't. They think this for two reasons – they have mortgaged their future already by buying things they didn't have the money for (living above their means) and they have no clue where their money is going.

This is where a spending plan helps. 90% of my clients come to me 2 or more months behind in their bills. I spend 30 minutes setting up a written spending plan for them and over 75% of the time I find $300 or more extra a month. So how did they get 2 or more months behind if they have extra money every month. You guessed right again – they didn't have a written plan as to where their money needed to go. When you do this, it will show you, literally, what you need for fixed expenses (items you have a commitment to pay every month) and then it will tell you whether you have enough to cover your obligations or not. If you don't, something has to give – either you need more money or you need to spend less. There is no money tree to help you out. And if you determine that you have money left over every month, you can decide where you want it to go instead of losing it month after month. When we don't have a written plan, we lose so much money. How many times have you looked up and wondered where the heck did my paycheck go?

Regular budgets are easy. You can use a spreadsheet, an app, or simply a pad and paper to do a written spending plan. If you have a regular income, simply put your income at the top, list all of your expenses and subtract. If that number is positive, you are in a positive position. If the number is negative, you need to make some immediate changes.

For those of you with irregular income, the steps are the same. You just need one additional step. You must prioritize your expenses. This will help you in the months where there is not enough money. You want to make sure you pay for housing, food, and utilities before anything else. And anytime you have extra, put it over into a savings account so that you will be able to cover all of your obligations every month without worry.

I'm going to be honest – I hate budgeting. But I realized a long time ago that my money was going where I told it and the best way to stay on the positive side of things was to write it down so that I had a visual. I learned to respect the money that God put me in charge of. I give first, pay myself next (save 10%) and live on the rest. Side note - whether you are a person of faith who tithes or not, giving to others is an important step to wealth as well. I never have to ask myself again, "where did my money go". I am in control of my finances and that has given me the financial freedom I so desired.

If you are scared or still not convinced of this budgeting thing, try it for six months. It's the only way that you will truly see if it works for you. I will promise you this one thing – you will feel freedom and control of your money like never before.

More Month Than Money

What happens when the month has 30 days, but you run out of money on the 20th?

"I have a serious problem that I don't know how to fix. Every month I run out of money in my checkbook before the month ends. I budget and I believe that I am a frugal person, but this happens every month. What can I do to stop this from happening?"

There are several issues in this one question that need to be addressed. In this particular question, the writer states that they do a budget. If you are having this problem and you are doing a budget, I encourage you to tweak what you are doing based on the last chapter. And of course, if you are not doing a budget, that is the first step to fixing this problem. If you don't know where your money is going or you are doing a budget in your head, odds are in your favor that you will run out of money before the month ends.

Now, let's assume that you are kicking butt in the budget department at this point having gotten this far in the book. Why else is your money running out and what can you do about it? Everything is going to come back to the budget because that is your blueprint for your income and your spending. If you are running out of money, odds are you aren't sticking 100% to the budget. Here are a few things that might be happening and how to make the necessary changes to your budget:

- **Spending more than budgeted in a category** – If you are running out of money before the end of the month, you may be spending more in a category than you are budgeting for. For example, maybe you budgeted $100 a month for gasoline and perhaps you drove more than usual or the price per gallon went up. You can't simply spend more and not make adjustments. If you need to spend more in one category, you must spend less in another. If you needed to spend $115 in gasoline one month, you would need to lower another category by $15. The point of a successful budget is to have a plan for every dollar that you bring in. That means that every dollar coming in has an assigned spot to go out – including savings, retirement, and unexpected expenses. Therefore, if you don't adjust your categories as the month goes along, you will run out of money before the end of the month.

- **Unrealistic numbers** – I always advise when starting a budget to do a spending journal for at least 3 months in conjunction with the budget. This will give you a realistic idea of where your money is actually going. And being real will help you to construct a budget that will work for you. Many wealthy people I know actually do a spending journal even now simply because they want to know where every dollar went. Being real will help you to succeed in the area of your finances every time.

- **G.O.K. category** – An older lady shared this category with me years ago and I have taught it ever since. It is the "God Only Knows" category. Every month you put a small amount - $20 - $40 – in this category and it covers small things that come up during the month that you didn't plan for. For me, it is always stamps. I never budget for them and all the sudden I need one and don't have one. With this category, I have what I need to buy the stamps without adjusting anything else. Anything you don't use up, you can carry over to the next month.

- **No umbrella for when it rains** – Doing everything we have talked about so far should make it where you never have more month than money. However, we all know that life happens and sometimes something happens that we just weren't expecting and couldn't budget for. This is where an emergency fund comes in. When something happens that you didn't budget for and you simply can't move money around between categories, you need an emergency fund that you can turn to. This will help you get through the current month and you can put the amount that you needed in the budget next month to replace what you used. I highly recommend a minimum of $1000, but anything in a savings account will help you through.

If you are having a problem with more month than money or it just happens once, look at everything you are doing and be honest with yourself in order to fix it. Remember a budget is not a punishment. It is a wealth building tool used to avoid financial problems just like this. Don't be afraid of it – embrace it. Use it to walk in your truth, make the necessary adjustments and continue your journey to wealth and financial freedom.

Emergency Fund – Why and How Big

"I hear all the time "save, save, save". You must have an emergency fund. Why do I need one? I use my credit cards as my emergency fund so I am always covered if something happens. Having my money just sitting there seems dumb especially if I never have an emergency."

I picked this particular question to address this issue because of how this follower deals with their emergencies. I get questions all the time about how big should my emergency fund be, and we will cover that in a moment, but every so often I get them asking why – why do I even need an emergency fund. So let me address that question first.

An emergency fund is simply money set aside in case of a rainy day. If you have an umbrella, you won't get soaked. However, if you don't, you will get drenched from head to toe and be extremely uncomfortable. That's all it is. The main reason you need one is that life happens. We have absolutely no way of predicting from one day to the next what is going to take place. However, we can be the eternal boy/girl scout and be prepared. The one thing I can promise you is that life will happen. You are not immune. I am a person of faith and I see miracles from God daily; however, I also have my share of emergencies. And that is because they are simply a part of life. If you have a car, odds are something will go wrong on it. If you have a house, odds are something will need to be repaired. Even if you rent and bike to work, you will still have emergencies – medical, job loss, etc. And when these things pop up, you need a way to pay for them.

Those of you who know me know I am cringing at the idea of using credit cards for emergencies. And here is why – it is not because credit cards are evil. They are simply a means of payment used to buy something. However, in this case, the absence of an emergency fund means you do not have the cash to pay for the emergency. Therefore, using your credit card for the emergency puts you into debt. Maybe you can pay it off in a few months and maybe it will be years. Either way, the fact that you don't have the cash means that you are going to be paying interest for that emergency. I would much rather make money in interest, i.e. my emergency fund, than I would pay money in interest, i.e. my credit cards.

Emergency funds are vital in order to avoid debt and build wealth. Having an emergency fund or savings set aside means that when something arises you can deal with it and move on. This will make the situation be an inconvenience and not a crippling event. This will bring you peace and not panic.

Having established, I hope, that an emergency fund is vital, let's talk numbers. If you don't have any savings at all, start somewhere. I would recommend at minimum $1000, but even $200 will help depending on the size of the emergency. Work extra, cut back spending, sell stuff – do whatever you need to do to save up quickly for a beginner emergency fund of at least $1000. Your long-term goal should be to have 6-8 months of expenses saved up. This amount has two purposes: It is large enough to cover big expenses such as home repairs and it is large enough to cover you in case of a job loss. Keep in mind, no job is guaranteed. In recent years, people found that out the hard way when they were losing jobs that they had had for over 20 years. No one, even the president of a company, is indispensable. Don't live your life in fear – simply plan ahead just in case and you can do your job in peace. You can never have too much money. The more you have, the more freedom you will have in the area of your finances. Just keep 6-8 months' worth of living expenses liquid so that you can get it if needed.

One thing I know about successful people that you will hear me say many times in this book is they plan. They have a plan for their money (a budget), they plan their lives (goals) and they plan for the unexpected (savings/emergency fund). It will rain – of that you can be sure. Have an umbrella ready and go singing in the rain!

Envelope System – Debit Cards vs. Cash

You will hear me say several times that personal finance is 10% math and 90% emotions. This formula is the reason why cash is always the best way to stay on budget especially if you are just starting the process.

"I use my debit card for all of my purchases – never a credit card. I am constantly hearing about the envelope system. Is this a better way for me to handle my spending? What are the advantages to both?"

Let me start by saying that not using credit cards is a great step forward in your financial journey. So many people put everything on a credit card with the intention of "dealing with it later". This can work for a few of the really disciplined people, but it doesn't work for most. Intentions are great, but reality can mess up even the best of intentions.

Now, to address whether debit cards or cash is better – you feel every purchase more when you pay with cash. And when you feel it, you will take that extra second to make a better decision. You will also spend less when using cash versus using a debit card. I know this seems odd – they are both a form of cash not credit. However, when all you have to do is swipe, you tend to spend more. When McDonald's introduced the credit card option to their restaurants, they did research and found that the average person spent at least 20% more when using a debit card versus cash.

The envelope system is the best system for helping you stay

on budget. And it is super simple. You don't need to buy a fancy wallet or anything – you can if it's easier. But really all you need are envelopes – either mailing envelopes or, my favorite, the free bank envelopes. Then you simply take every category that is not a fixed expense and you take the cash out of the bank and put it in the envelopes. Below are a few examples of the categories that are great to use the envelope system with:

- Groceries

- Eating Out

- Entertainment

- Gas

- Gifts

- Clothes

- Home repair

- Health and beauty items

- Supplies

Basically anything that isn't paid using a check or online payment.

What is great about this system is you have what you have and that is it. Let's say you budgeted $200 a month for groceries. If all you have is $200 in cash in an envelope, you are going to pay super close attention to every item you buy. You are going to meal plan and make a list. You will take the time to check your pantry and fridge for what you already have. Basically, you will pay attention more using cash because once it is gone, it is gone and there is no more until the next payday.

When you use a debit card, you tend to not pay as close attention. You figure if you go over by a little it doesn't matter. However, going over a little every time can add up quickly and throw your budget off. You will then need to figure out where to get the money to cover it until payday leaving the temptation to use credit cards as a strong possibility.

Both debit cards and cash are great methods of payment. And as I said, both are definitely better than credit cards. But with emotions playing such a large role in the money game, I highly recommend using the envelope system for all non-fixed items in your budget. This way, you will be able to stick to your budget and not have to constantly move money around between categories and risk coming up short at the end of the month. Try it. See how simple it is and I bet you will save money your first month. What do you have to lose?

Need vs. Want

"So many times, I have trouble just meeting my needs. If I can't meet my needs, how will I ever have stuff I want? What steps can I take to not only meet my needs, but to also get things and do what I want?"

The most common problem in personal finance is discerning what a true need is versus a want. Now, let me say before we get started that you can have both. But so many people, including myself, use the word "need" a little too freely. For example, you may say all the time "I need a haircut." You don't really need one. You won't die if you don't get a haircut. Your hair is just longer than you like it or longer than the style you like. If you were in a financial pinch and had to choose between food and a haircut, I hope you would choose food everytime. I found out in my financial journey that even a washer and dryer were wants. Most people have them, but you can function without them. Many of our grandparents did. Is life easier with them, absolutely, but if yours broke down and you didn't have the money to get new ones, you could find a way. You could hand wash your clothes and hang them up to dry. Convenient? No, but it definitely could be done.

Again, let me reiterate – you can have both needs and wants if your finances allow, but being real about needs versus wants will help you have a different perspective and in the long run save you money. I believe that your goal should be to have both, but it is crucial that you meet your true needs first and then address your wants. Let's look at some of the common misconceptions when it comes to true needs versus wants:

- You need shelter – you want a 2000 square foot home with a renovated kitchen. We all need a roof over our head, but you can live in a studio apartment if that is all your budget will allow. You can have roommates if necessary. If you are having trouble meeting this need or even if you are house poor, take a serious look at this category and consider making a serious change until you are in a better financial place.

- You need food – you want to eat out. Again, we all need food, but we could live on Raman noodles if we had to. Many people tell me that they can't live on less than $100 a week for food for 2 people. However, I live on $50-60 a week and that includes eating out once. It can be done. When you are in a crisis, you may not be able to afford steak, or name brand items. You definitely can't afford to eat out. But you can meet your need for food.

- You need clothes – you don't need a walk-in closet full. This is one that gets people in trouble a lot. If you have enough clothes for one week and a good pair of shoes, you have your clothes needs met. Above and beyond that is want. This goes for purses too. No one lady needs 5 purses. I have 3 and it is 3 more than I need. I could carry my stuff in a bag of any type. I know this seems extreme to some of you, but you need to get honest about this and also to realize how blessed you already are.

- You need transportation – you don't need a car. In most cities and towns, there are many ways to get around. And there are many modes of transportation like bicycles and walking. Yes, cars are great and they get us places faster. I have two cars and I know that I am blessed beyond blessed. But if you truly didn't have the money, you could find a way.

And that is what this whole exercise is about. I found myself 20 years ago not having the money for some of these items. And I sure as heck didn't have the credit to go get them. So I learned a different way. And in learning a different way, it has made me more and more grateful for everything I do have and I am able to be honest with myself about the fact that I have a lot of wants. And to take it one step further – cable, internet and cell phones are wants. We lived a great life without them in the 70's and 80's and you can live without them now.

If you are still reading this chapter, kudos. Most people don't like to hear the truth when it comes to this stuff. But here is why I say this. Odds are you can meet your true needs. Some can't and for those people there are organizations to help you like our ministry, Lovell Ministries and so many others. But when you realize what your true needs are, you can put life and your finances in a different perspective. To the lady who wrote the question in the beginning of this chapter – I challenged her to address her true needs first and then her wants. When you do this, you will find areas where you can cut back and sacrifice in order to have and do the things that are most important to you. Most people don't have the ability to have everything they want instantly. Once you meet your true needs, sit down and look at your wants and see what is most important to you. Maybe you can get by with one car in order to travel. Maybe you sacrifice cable in order to have a cell phone. Maybe you buy less clothes in order to eat out occasionally. When you really get the needs versus wants concept, your options are endless.

What is Debt, Really?

You would think a word like debt would have only one meaning. However, depending on who you ask, you will likely get multiple definitions. This is because people don't like to think they are in debt. Being is debt is not as simple as you have a bill that needs to be paid. So let's dive into the true meaning of debt and how to determine if you are in debt or not.

"I have a car payment and a mortgage. Someone told me I was not debt free because of this. However, I only owe $100,000 on the house which is worth $150,000 and $15,000 on the car which is worth $8,000 and I have over $300,000 in an retirement account. Am I in debt or not?"

No, this lady is not in debt. Debt is owing more than you have and she doesn't. At anytime she can write a check and be payment free (which I would recommend), but many wealthy people choose this route because they pay 3-4% using someone else's money where they would pay 12% or more to use theirs. This would be the case if the money they have is in a growth stock mutual fund or some investment that is making an average return.

Let's start from the beginning. As I said, debt is simply owing more than you have. The way to determine this is to know your net worth (which we will cover in more detail later). Your net worth – simply speaking – is the total of your assets minus the total of what you owe. Let's look at the example above. She has assets of $458,000 and she owes $115,000. Therefore, she is not in debt. She has simply chosen to use the banks money instead of her own. But at anytime, she could write a check and be payment free.

Now, even though she is not in debt, she is however, a slave to her lenders (Proverbs 22:7). She owes people money every month at a certain time and continues to run the risk of them changing the rules at any moment. Based on the biblical principle in Proverbs 22:7, I would highly recommend that she pay everyone what she owes and release the shackles that they have placed on her. Owing no one is the greatest feeling in the world and gives you great potential because your income is your greatest wealth building tool. When parts of your income aren't promised to others, you can use it to quickly build wealth.

I want to share a part of my story that I hope will help you when trying to decide whether to use your assets to pay off everything or to hold on to your payments. There was a time when I had become 100% debt free – owing no one anything. After that, I began to build my assets up through retirement and mutual fund accounts. At some point, I began to start getting credit card offers and before I knew it, I had several credit cards with great reward programs. This was not the problem. I then began to buy things using these cards and paying them in full. Again, not the problem. Then as time went on, I started charging more than I had cash for. Now, I was never in debt – I was still debt free. However, I now had several additional monthly payments that had to be made every month and since I was growing my business, I wasn't always able to pay them in full. So even though I technically wasn't in debt, I was a slave to my payments. This began to get stressful for me – the same feeling I had when I was in debt. I wasn't about to cash out my retirement to pay these cards; therefore, I was saddled with the stress of the monthly payment. I had the asset to cover the debt if needed, but not the liquidity to pay cash and remove the middle man altogether. Needless to say, I paid everything off as quick as possible and never got caught on that wheel again.

How you pay for things is a personal choice and I know many people who use credit cards and pay them in full every month. And as long as you can stay off the payment wheel, I don't see the harm. However, many of us get caught up in the wheel and before we know it, owe more than we have in cash (even if we have the asset to back it up).

Your first goal should be to evaluate your net worth. In doing so, if you find out you are in debt, develop a plan to pay it off completely (which we will address later on). If you are not in debt, but have monthly payments of some kind, I would challenge you to pay off these items as quickly as possible and get off the payment wheel. Knowing you have no debt – the assets are more than the expenses – can give you a great piece of mind in your finances. But I truly believe that jumping off the payment wheel will bring you a peace beyond anything else when it comes to your money. I took the leap and I hope you will too.

The 411 on Credit Cards

"I have heard so many money experts say credit cards are bad and we should never use them. But some of them have great rewards. What is so bad and why do experts say to never use them?"

First of all, let me say that credit cards are not evil and credit card companies are not the devil. I have actually partnered with some of the top companies like Capital One, Chase and Discover to educate people in the area of their money. But you are right – many of my colleagues believe that you should never have a card and if you do, you are stupid. And this is simply not true.

I learned two big lessons in my journey: Personal finance is personal and knowledge is power. And credit cards encompass both of those items. They are a personal choice, but using them correctly is vital to your financial well-being. Let's take a look at this second part first.

Credit cards are simply a form of payment – just like debit cards and cash. If you want to purchase something, you are given 2-4 choices of payment (cash, check, debit card or credit card). 3 of these 4 means of payment come straight out of your checking account – cash on demand. The 4th option requires you borrowing money that you have been pre-approved for. Even if you pay off the bill in full every month, you are still borrowing from that company from the time you swipe until the time you pay.

When you use your cash on hand (cash, check or debit card), you feel it. It makes you pay attention to what you are buying and helps you stay on course with your budgeting. Paying this way is immediate – the results are immediate. The merchant will take the cash immediately out of your account; therefore, allowing little wiggle room for error. This makes you pay attention. No one wants to overdraft their account or realize at checkout that you don't have enough. So, you keep up. I check my checking account every day. I want to make sure that I know exactly what is going on in order to avoid any mishap. Nowadays the only mishap would be identity theft and someone wiping the account out, but when I was living paycheck to paycheck, one mistake, sometimes of even just $5, would overdraft my account. Suddenly my $5 latte cost me $40. When I began getting out of debt, I went to the envelope system, using cash for everything but my fixed bills. We have already talked about that and why it works so well. Today, I could pay with whatever form of payment I want; however, I still use a cash system (literal dollars) to pay for everything that is not fixed or bought online. Even though my amounts are bigger, it still makes me pay attention and stay on budget – eliminating impulse purchases and bringing out my patience as sometimes I have to wait until the next month to get what I want.

Now that I have given you what I do, let me address credit cards for those who want to use them for the rewards. First of all, let me remind you of what we talked about in the last chapter. Credit cards not paid in full every single month results in interest charges (paying extra for your purchases) and can result in debt if you owe more than you have. This is never ok – meaning this will never bring you wealth. The only way to become wealthy is to spend less than you make. Otherwise, you will never have anything to save or invest which will result in no cushion, no money for the future, and stress.

As for credit cards themselves, let's look at the good and the bad. The good things about credit cards are that most of them have a reward system attached to them: cash rewards, statement credits, travel points, etc. If you really want to take advantage of these rewards and decide to get a credit card, I want to take a moment to let you know the risks.

There is always a risk when borrowing money from others – even for a short time. Sometimes life can throw us curve balls and if you owe people money, you can end up behind without expecting it. A huge lesson I learned was that my intentions didn't always meet my reality. And because of this I needed to make decisions where this wasn't an issue. And borrowing money was a big area for me with this. If I don't owe anyone anything on a daily basis, when life throws me a curve ball, I can just hit it out of the park – no worries.

If you choose to use a credit card to pay for items throughout the month, and again, it is a personal choice, let me warn you of one more thing so that you don't mess up your credit report (your financial reputation). Most credit card companies report on a monthly basis to the 3 credit bureaus. They report your payment standing, your minimum payment amount and your balance. The balance that they report is your statement balance. This can highly affect your credit score in a negative way even if you pay in full every month. Let me explain.

One of the top factors of your credit score is credit utilization (30%). This is the percentage of your credit limit that you have used. For example, if your balance is $500 and your credit limit is $1000, then your utilization would be 50%. Now, here is the part that can really mess you up even if you pay in full. Let's say you charged $800 on a card that had $1000 limit. Your statement balance is $800 and that is what will be reported. Therefore, your utilization will be 80% even if you pay if full every month. You want it to be under 30% with 10% boosting your score even more. There is a way to avoid this if you are choosing to use a credit card. Make sure to pay the balance and have it posted before the statement date. For example, if your statement date is the 15th of every month, make sure you pay it off by the 10th (earlier if mailing a payment). This way, you will show a $0 balance each and every month even though you are using the card and gaining the rewards. This does mean paying your bill way before it is due; however, it is the only way to keep your credit score accurate to your reality.

I hope that this gives you a clearer picture of credit cards. Again, they are not evil and if you are in debt, the cards are not your issue – the way you used them is. My colleagues who teach absolutely no credit cards mean well. Most of them, like me, have had a bad experience with them. But again, the problems were not the credit cards themselves. The problem was our thinking about money that happened to show up in the form of credit card balances. Credit cards are the easiest way to buy something that you want now even though you don't have the money and that is the real issue – impatience and spending more than you make.

I pray that you now have a clear picture of how each payment method works and based on the knowledge you have gained, you can make the best decision that works for you and your future. And if you make the decision to use a credit card, please pay in full every month before the statement date or don't use them at all.

Everyone Else is Doing It

For the next few chapters we are going to cover everything you need to know about getting out of debt. The Bible says to owe nothing to anyone but the obligation to love (Romans 13:8); therefore, if you are a person of faith, having debt is being disobedient to God. I am not judging – remember I was there with 5 zeros – I'm just being honest because many Christians have convinced themselves that debt is okay.

"I was told growing up that debt was a part of life. In order to drive a car, own a house, travel, pretty much anything required debt. However, owing all this money makes me very anxious. Is debt a given in life or should I work on getting out of debt?"

This is a common question as most people are taught debt is okay and just a part of life. I cringe every time I hear the phrase "good debt". There is nothing positive about debt. There is no debt that is "good". Many people look at student loans and mortgages as good debt. Student loans are bad debt - you can invest in your future and get the school you need with cash as we will talk about later. And a mortgage has an asset to back it up if done properly which we will also talk about later. Remembering our definition of debt, debt is never okay.

If you have debt, you should definitely work on paying it all off and going to a cash based system. If you don't have the money, then don't buy it. It is that simple. Many times I am asked "why should I get out of debt". We have already covered why if you are a person of faith – because God clearly says to owe no one and there are no exceptions to this.

But even if you are not a person of faith or perhaps you are a believer who isn't always obedient because it means giving up your "fun", there are many reasons why you should get out of debt. Let me ask you this – and this is for people of faith and others – is being in debt making you happy? I mean truly happy. Are you finding joy and peace in your debt? If you are, by all means keep it. I can say that because I know the answer is no.

God doesn't tell us to not owe anyone because He is mean or doesn't want us to have what we want. He says to owe no one because He knows what it can do to our joy and peace. Remember Proverbs 22:7 – "The borrower is slave to the lender."? He says this multiple times because He loves us so much, He doesn't want something like owing money to steal our joy and our peace.

So, let me sum it up for you – Debt is a stressful thing. Owing others and having that monthly financial obligation and that balance hanging around is robbing you of your peace and your future dreams. The only way to reach financial peace and freedom and build wealth is to pay off all – yes, I said all – of your debt. This will take time, it will take patience and it will take sacrifice and in some cases, major life changes, but it is worth all of it.

Now that I have covered the why, let me just say this in answer to the other part of the question. Debt is not a given. My grandparents never had debt. My parents never had debt. The reason so many people have accepted debt as a given is because we have convinced ourselves that we "must" have what we want when we want it. And the banks have given us the means to do just that.

One of my favorite things to teach millennials is how to buy a new car with cash. (I will share this with you in a future chapter.) I love to see that look on their face when they realize that they can pay cash for a new car. Everything can we cash flowed, even things like student loans and houses. I went to college debt free and so are many of other crazy people. It can be done. It is all about choice and patience.

Take it from someone who has been there – I had $200,000 worth of debt 20 years ago – if you are in debt, do everything you need to do to get out. If you are young and have no debt, keep it that way. There is absolutely nothing you need or want that is worth your joy and peace. And if you take the time, you can figure out how to get everything you want and need with cash. I do it every day and so can you!

Cleaning Up The Past

Okay, so now let's assume you have "bought in" to everything we have talked about so far and you have decided to live a no debt lifestyle. If you are like me, odds are you have a past that you will need to clean up somewhere along the way.

"I am trying to become debt free, but I am not sure where to start. I have current debts that I am paying on, but in addition to those, I have past debts that are in collections. How do I deal with these when I don't have the money right now to pay them off?"

This is a great question and something, that if not done properly, can come back to haunt you. Your first priority is to make sure that all current accounts are kept up to date. In a couple of chapters, we will talk about the different ways to pay off current debt and what is best for you, but making sure that nothing else goes into collections is extremely important.

Once you pay everything off that is current you can begin to clean up your past. You want to picture your old debts as sleeping bears. As long as they are sleeping, you don't want to do anything to wake them up. And when you are ready, you begin to wake them up one at a time.

When you are ready to wake the bear, you want to reach out to them in writing and let them know that you would like to make an offer of "settlement in full". Saying it this way is vital because you want to make sure that the amount you pay will clear the account forever. Most times, depending on how long an account has been out there and depending on the type of account, an account can be cleared for 25 -50 cents on the dollar. This means that if you owe $1000, odds are you can make them an offer of $250 - $500 in cash and settle the account. So, the first step is to talk to them, call or send a letter, and make them an offer. Next, is to make sure that you get the offer in writing, either in email form or in letter form. You **must** have the offer in writing with the condition of the account being settled in full before you settle the account. If a company won't do that or they want more than you have, simply let them know you can't do it right now and move on to the next one. Never let them bully you. You owe the money and you need to settle with them, but you must make sure you do it properly or it will come back later.

Once you have the offer in writing, send them a money order or cashier's check. Never give them your bank information – verbally or in the form of a personal check. You don't want to take the risk of them cleaning out your account. Then you simply take a copy of the letter or email, attach a copy of the money order or cashier's check to it and keep it forever – and I really mean forever. Companies are constantly buying old debts even ones that have been settled and they try to collect again. Without written proof, you won't be able to defend your case and you may end up paying twice. Many collectors are reputable and straight up, but many are not and you need to protect yourself from the ones who are not.

Every so often, as you are trying to get out of debt, a bear will wake up on its own. When it does, you need to take care of it as quickly as possible in order to keep it calm. Work them into your getting out of debt plan as quick as you can, even if it means slowing down something else, and get them out of the way. Try not to ignore them if possible because you don't want to create a bigger problem in the future.

Lastly, sometimes a debt is large enough and the company is big enough that they will file to get a judgement against you. Don't panic and in most cases, there is not a need for a lawyer. Feel free to check with one based on the letter you receive, but I definitely wouldn't panic. This is a common procedure in this type of scenario.

When you receive a summons regarding the intent to sue, let the case go through. You can show up or not – if you don't have the money, the result will be the same; a judgement will be placed against you. At that time, a lawyer will be assigned to the case and you will be able to work with them in order to settle the case. You want to settle it using the same procedure we just talked about.

The biggest thing when it comes to debt is owning that you owe it. You spent the money and weren't able to repay it. This is not the bank's fault – it is yours. You wrote checks your butt couldn't cover and now that you realize that isn't a good plan, you can take the steps necessary for you to fix it. And as we have talked about, you should be able to settle most old debts (debts in collections) for less that you actually owe which is a blessing. I highly recommend clearing up as many debts as you can. It will lessen your chances of the past haunting you forever and you will be able to experience true financial peace.

To File or Not To File

So many times we believe that there is only one, at most two, solutions for every problem. If that's all you see, you aren't thinking outside the box enough. This is the way it is with bankruptcy – to file or not to file; that is the question.

"It looks like I am going to need to file bankruptcy in order to get my finances in order. I have about $80,000 in debt, of which $50,000 is student loans and the rest is medical and credit cards. I can't see how I am ever going to pay these off. I feel like bankruptcy is my only answer. Please help."

Bankruptcy has always been the answer when it comes to starting over in our finances. We get in over our heads and we decide to file bankruptcy and clear the slate. But there are many questions that need to be addressed before deciding to file for bankruptcy and in most cases, a simple restructuring is all we really need.

10 years ago, filing for bankruptcy was easy and the answer for so many consumers when they found themselves drowning in debt. However, over the last few years, the laws have changed and have made it much more difficult to even file bankruptcy, which is a good thing. I can't say that there is never a time when bankruptcy is the answer, but I can say that about 90% of the time (or more), it is not.

First of all, let's address what cannot be put into a bankruptcy. Student loans and IRS debt are not bankruptable. This means, in our sample question, only $30,000 of the $80,000 can be included in a bankruptcy. Knowing that paints a completely different picture.

Now, most debt that can be included in a bankruptcy can also be paid off with some sort of payment plan or even some type of settlement agreement which we just talked about. What this means is that if the $30,000 in our sample question is old debt, odds are it could be settled for around $15,000. So we just took an $80,000 bankruptcy down to a $15,000 problem.

Look, I get it. When you can't see the light at the end of the tunnel, you want to just do what seems easy and file for bankruptcy and wipe the slate clean. Your credit is already bad so what is 7 more years, right? And filing for bankruptcy makes for a clean slate to make better decisions on. I really do get it. But consider how much better it would be if you were able to work through your debt yourself.

The greatest thing that ever happened to me was working my way out of debt. I know that doesn't make sense, but hear me out. I had horrible money habits. That is how I got in the situation I was in – spending more than I made, needing everything right away, doing just enough to get by. And if someone would have come and waved a magic wand over my debt and made it go away, guess what? I would have done the exact same thing again. The reason is my situation changed, but my mindset and my habits didn't. By working my way through my debt, I learned, over time, a whole new way to handle money. I learned patience, I learned sacrifice, I learned to work hard. I learned that some things I had to do were for a season, but some things I had to do were for a lifetime. And those things are bringing me a lifetime of wealth and financial freedom, not just a season of it.

Filing for bankruptcy is harder than it looks. It will leave scars, deep scars, that will take a long time to heal. I highly recommend that you look at every option before you even consider filing. I know that for some of you, bankruptcy may be the answer and there is absolutely no judgment there, not from me at least. I just want to make sure you know all of your options before taking such a big, life altering step. Whether you file or you don't, you will come through this and my prayer is that you come through it with new habits, a new outlook and a whole new financial situation (for the better).

Just let me reiterate – IRS debt and student loans cannot be included in a bankruptcy. All other debts – credit cards, medical bills, personal loans, auto loans, etc. – can be worked out through settlement plans with the companies, collection agency or the lawyers assigned to your case (depending on how far the process has gone). These people will try to threaten you at times and try to scare you into paying whatever they say, but know your rights. Just remain calm, cool and collected, lay out a plan and only file for bankruptcy as a final option and only when there is no other way.

Snowball vs. Avalanche

"I am ready to get out of debt, but I am not sure which one to pay off first. I hear people say pay it off smallest to largest, but then others say pay off the highest interest first. Which way is best?"

First of all, let me say that the decision to pay off debt is the most important thing. Paying down debt, no matter which method you choose, is a great thing. The next thing that is important is making sure that you stay motivated through the process. Therefore, which method you choose – the debt snowball, the debt avalanche, or your own concoction, only matters to the extent that you don't give up. Let's take a look at both methods and discuss their pros and their cons so that you can make an informed decision.

Debt snowball – The snowball method is simply paying off your debts smallest to largest. This is the most popular because you can see results the fastest. Here is how it works: you make a list of all of your debts – smallest to largest. Every month you make the minimum payments on all of them and throw all of the extra money at the smallest one. Then you take the minimum payment from that one after it's paid off, add it to the next one and repeat the process. As you pay off each debt, your monthly "snowball" (minimum payment) gets bigger and bigger. If the minimum payment on your first debt was $25, when you pay it off you then add the $25 to the next minimum payment, let's say it's $25 and now you are putting at least $50 on the next debt plus any extra. By the time you are a few debts in, your minimum on your smallest debt can be $100 or more – knocking the debt out even quicker.

Debt avalanche – The avalanche method is simply paying off debt in the order of the higher interest rate. It is similar to the snowball in that you pay the minimum on all of them, throwing all extra money at the one with the highest interest rate. And when you get one paid off, you take that minimum and add it to the next one, raising your monthly minimum on the one you are focused on.

The snowball method is great because you can see the progress quickly. I have had clients who started their snowball at the same time they started budgeting and with extreme focus and sacrifice, they were able to pay off two or three debts in one month. This is great if you are a visual person – if you need to see continued progress in order to not give up.

The avalanche method can be an issue visually because your first debt to pay off might be $5,000 or more. This means it will be awhile before you can see even one debt gone. However, if the math is more important and you can stay motivated, the avalanche method will work for you.

I will be transparent – I used the snowball method for the most part, but I did move a few debts around for my own peace of mind. As I said in the beginning, the most important thing is that you do what is going to work for you. Personal finance is personal and something that worked for someone else may not work for you. And that's ok.

For both methods, or any method you design for yourself,

you want to make sure that every time you pay a debt off, you use that minimum for the next one. Paying off a debt doesn't free up more money to buy stuff. It, along with every dollar you can find, needs to be used to get yourself out of debt.

Let me share just a few success stories I came across recently to show you it can be done if you want it bad enough.

Dallas and Sami - $195,000 in 18 months

Mel - $25,000 in 6 months

Debbie - $30,274.04 in 23 months

Jessica - $153,217 in 6 ½ years

Angela and Jeff - $58,700 in 2 years

Lisa - $39,000 in 48 months

Mark and Emily - $24,000 in less than 1 year

James and Aimee - $136,000 in 47 months

Stephanie and her husband - $144,064 in less than 3 years

Stacy and Barry - $20,000 in 8 months

There is a lot of variety here between amounts and time frame. But they all have something in common. They did it and they never gave up! And you can too. It doesn't matter how big your number is – mine was $200,000 – what matters is how bad you want it and what are you going to do to get it. I hope you want it really bad and you are willing to do what it takes for a short while to live an awesome life for the long haul. Use the method that works for you and go kick some debt butt!

Is My 401K an Option?

This is a question that is asked almost daily, but has one simple answer. Here we go!

"I am developing my get out of debt strategy and I wanted to know should I use the $25,000 in my 401K to pay off most of my debt. If I do this, I can be debt free in about 6 months."

This is a question that seems like the answer would change based on the scenario, but it doesn't. The answer is always no – no matter what amount you have in the 401K or how much debt you have. And here is why.

First, when you take money out of your 401K you not only have to pay tax on it, you also have to pay a penalty if you are not 59 ½. Most of you are probably in the 20-25% tax bracket and the penalty is 10%. So this would be like paying off debt with an interest rate of 30%. You would never do that. You have to realize that your 401K or any retirement plan you have is not free money. There is always a cost for using it and if you are not of retirement age, the cost is substantial. For this reason alone, the answer is always no.

But there are other reasons to consider as well. This money is making money. It was set in place so that when you retire, you will have some money to live on. You have already mortgaged some of your future by accumulating the debt in the first place. You have spent future earnings for something you wanted today – earnings that you have no promise of ever collecting. You don't want to mortgage even more of your future by using your retirement to pay off the debt. Just like bankruptcy, it can seem like a harmless, easy solution, when in fact it can have major future repercussions. You want to make sure that every decision you make going forward is a positive step not only for the moment, but for your future as well.

While we are on the subject of 401K's let me address another part to this question. Many people want to know about taking a 401K loan out to pay off their debt since the interest rate on this type of loan is low and you are technically paying it to yourself and not a bank.

A 401K loan is never a good idea. Yes, you are paying yourself, but if you lose your job for any reason, the balance of the loan is considered a withdrawal and comes with all of the fees we spoke about earlier – the tax implication and the early withdrawal fee. You may think your job is secure, but I promise you it is only as secure as the next minute. I don't say that to be negative, but many of us fall into this false sense of security that our company will always be around and so will our job. Just this week, GE laid off 12,000 people. I am sure all of them thought their job was secure because, well, it's GE. You don't need to be negative, but you do need to understand things can happen and you need to prepare for them. If you knew you were going to lose your job, you would never consider a 401K loan. And since you have no idea what the next 3-5 years are going to bring, you want to err on the side of caution and find another option.

Plus, think of all of the money you will be losing – free money in growth – while you are paying back that loan. If your loan was taken out in the last year or two, you would have lost substantial free money just in growth alone. You will definitely be losing more than the 5% you are paying yourself back in interest.

I will say it one more time. Always do the math and always look beyond today to see how your decisions will affect your future. If you do that anytime you are thinking about using your 401K to pay off debt, whether in the form of a withdrawal or a loan, you will definitely see where these are not good options. I really do appreciate that you are looking at every possible option to get out of debt as quickly as possible and if these were individual stocks or just regular mutual funds, it might be a different answer. But there are just too many cons to using your 401K to pay off your debt.

All Hands on Deck

"I want to be out of debt so bad. What are some things I can do to speed up the process? I am ready and willing to do what it takes, but I'm just not sure where to start."

I love people like this. People who are what some describe as "gazelle intense" – putting everything they've got into getting out of debt. For them it is not just a distant dream – it is a life goal with a specific date. People with this kind of mindset and intensity will get out of debt quicker than what any calculator can predict.

If you are one of these people, let me share many things that you can do to speed up the process.

> **Extra gigs** – This means doing any type of work to bring in extra money. It can be an extra part time job, stepping up your hobby game, working from home, etc. This can look like anything from dog walking to mowing lawns, selling on Etsy to becoming a virtual assistant. In this internet age, you literally have the world at your fingertips.

> **Lower your bills** – You can lower any bill that you have if you want to including your rent/mortgage. Take a serious look at all of your bills and see where you can cut back. I went from $400 a month in groceries to $240. We upped our deductible on our auto insurance to $1000 once we had our emergency fund. Odds are you are paying for things you aren't

using and you are definitely paying for things you don't need. Lower or get rid of your cable bill, go to a prepaid cell phone, stop eating out, rent movies instead of going to the theatre. There are so many things that you can do if you want to get out of debt bad enough and remember this – everything is just for a short season. As soon as you pay off the debt, you will have more money and you will be able to budget cable, eating out, movies, etc.

Sell anything and everything – Now is a great time to look at what you have and ask yourself "does it bring value to my life?" If the answer is no, sell it. Have a huge garage sale, post your items to local sites, or use eBay – whatever path is best for the item you are selling. As you pay off debt, you will find that your "stuff" brings you less value than that feeling of being debt free and having financial freedom. Be honest about the last time you used something and bring value to someone else's life by selling it to someone who really wants it.

Downsize – Now we are going to get super radical and I know this may not be for everyone. But I have to put it out there because I have had clients do this and be very happy and successful. If you have a car loan, sell the car and buy yourself something cheaper. If you are upside down on the loan, this won't get you completely out from under it, but you will be in much better shape than you are now. For example, let's say you owe $16,000 on a car that is worth $14,000. You sell it for $14,000 and get a small personal loan from a credit union for the $2,000 you are short plus another $3,000 or so to get a decent used car. Doing this means you are $5,000 in debt on a car instead of $16,000. You just paid off $11,000 of your debt. You can also do this on your home if your house payment is just killing you and preventing you from moving forward. Again, downsizing is radical, but can move you forward very quickly when it comes to larger loans like cars and houses.

Found money – I would definitely put any extra money I received – an inheritance, a bonus at work, a tax refund (which we will address later) – anything that comes to you unexpectedly, take it and pay down your debt.

As you can see there are a lot of things you can do to speed up the getting out of debt process. And I've only named a few. The real question isn't what to do, but how fast do I want to do it and that is something that only you can decide. I highly recommend sacrificing big time now in order to get out of debt as quickly as possible. Then use your income to build wealth. Start making interest instead of paying it.

Repairing the Problem

"I have had several repairs on my car over the last few months. How do I know when to repair the problem and when it is time to get a new one?"

If I had a nickel for every time I heard "I need a new car", I would never have to work again. New cars are fun especially nowadays with all of the awesome technology, but they are not always the best decision for you. I am not one of those money people who will tell you to never buy a new car unless you are a millionaire; however, I will tell you in the next two chapters how to pay cash for a new car and how to buy one without hurting your future plans.

We must understand that cars are a depreciating asset and they begin depreciating the moment you drive them off the car lot. We all have the reality that we are going to need some type of transportation expense in our budget, but how much and how we do it needs to be in conjunction with our financial snapshot.

In addressing the question of whether to repair or whether to buy, you must first look at your financial snapshot. If you have debt or will go into debt to purchase a different car whether new or used, the answer is always going to be repair. Our goal is to get out of debt and stay out or simply never go into debt depending on where you are financially. With that goal in mind, the answer to your situation is never going to be to use debt.

Now, if you have the money to repair your car in your emergency fund and the repair is less than the value of the vehicle, you will definitely want to repair the car. If it is not, you may want to consider a different car that you can pay cash for – using your emergency fund and any money you can get for your current vehicle. And to answer your next question, yes there are always people willing to pay $500 or so for vehicles that don't work. You will want to check out salvage yards and places like that. There is always a small value to any car in the working parts. However, if you really love your car, you can fix it for now and keep it. For most repairs on older cars, either way is okay.

Now what happens when a large car part breaks such as an engine or transmission? Or perhaps you live in a state like I do that has inspections and your car will no longer pass. When something like this happens, you will need to find a nice used car to buy based on the funds you have available. And by funds available, I mean cash on hand or perhaps money you can get by selling something. I do not mean the amount a bank will loan you. Again, get what you can from salvaging your current vehicle and add it to the cash on hand and buy something reliable.

I know that driving used cars can be tedious at times. I also know that it can be challenging to find a good, reliable car for a low price. But as we have talked about so many times already, you want to avoid taking what appears to be the easy way out by financing a new car. This may seem like the answer, but it will only make your already large hole even bigger.

A great tip for finding a reliable used car that has worked for me many times is looking for a car that hasn't been driven a lot and is well taken care of. You will usually find this type of car being sold by older people or perhaps at estate sales. Avoid the "buy here, pay here" lots and the car lots around town that have older cars. Ask around or look on local selling sites and try to find a good, reliable, inexpensive car. It may not look pretty, but it will be the best thing for you.

There is a time and place to buy a new car and there is a way to cash flow it which we will talk about in the next chapter. However, don't panic when you have a car repair and buy one out of desperation. There is always a solution. It might not be immediate and it might not be obvious, but it is there. I actually learned how to deal with car issues years ago when I was getting out of debt and building my emergency fund. I didn't always have a lot of cash sitting around, but I also didn't have access to credit at the time as I had ruined my credit and was in the process of rebuilding it. This meant I could only do what I am telling you. I am grateful that I didn't have other options because I am sure at that place in that time, I would have gotten a car loan and it would have had at least an 18% interest rate. That would have set me way back in my debt free journey. I know if you have a car repair and just a starter emergency fund (or even less), it can be overwhelming. Just step back, look at all of your options and figure out which one is going to move you forward in your wealth journey, not backwards.

Buying a New Car with Cash

Many of you probably think this is only possible if you are wealthy, but the average person could never do this. That is simply not true. Anyone can pay cash for a new car – from a 21-year-old new college graduate to a 65 year old retiree.

"I really want a new car, but there is no way I can ever save to pay cash for it. I always hear that car loans are considered "good debt". Is that true? Isn't it pretty much a given that you will always have a car loan?"

Society, as a whole, believes exactly what this person was saying. Most people believe that they will always have a car loan because it is the only way to buy a car – new or used. But I am here to tell you this is simply not true. And as we talked about already, there is no "good debt". That is an oxymoron.

I will never forget when I shared what I am about to share with you to a group of recent college graduates. One girl sat there in amazement at something so simple and said to me "Where were you 2 years ago?" She had graduated college, had student loan debt, had life expenses and on top of that, had added a car loan. She literally thought there was no other way. She didn't have any money; therefore, to her, it wasn't about cash. It was all about the monthly payment. If you live your life saying "How much is the monthly payment", you will never build wealth. Wealthy people look at the total cost and not just how much per month.

Now, before I show you my secret formula (it's not really a secret), let me share a few mind blowing statistics that I hope will convince you to never have a car loan again. As of the writing of this book, the average car payment is $479. If you take that car payment and invest it from age 25-65, in just an average growth stock mutual fund, you will have $2.8 million. I'm not kidding – put it in any investment calculator and you will get the same number. And I even low balled it because the average return over 30 years in a growth stock mutual fund is 12% and I only did 10%. Maybe your car payment is only $300 a month. Well, that will net you $1.8 million in the same time frame. Do you see why wealthy people don't have a car payment? They choose to invest their money and let it make money instead of paying extra for something they can eventually pay cash for.

So let's look at a simple way to pay cash for a new car.

Year 1 – Buy a $2,000.00 car for cash. This means finding a good estate sale car that will work for you for a short time. During the year, set aside a car payment into a savings account – whatever amount you would have paid if you bought the new car now.

Year 2 – Sell your $2,000 car and buy a $5600.00 car. This is simply the $2,000 you got from selling your car (it's only one year older so you should be able to get the same price or close) and the $3,600 you saved (assuming a low car payment of $300).

Year 3 – Sell your $5,600 car and buy a $9,200 car. Same formula as year two.

Year 4 – Sell your $9,200 car and buy a $12,800 car.

Year 5 – Sell your $12,800 car and buy a new car for $16,400.

Yippee! You did it!

Now, let's look at why you want to do it this way and not take out a loan.

- You will pay $18,755 for a $16,400 car if you take out a loan. And that is at a 5% interest rate, which means odds are it will be more.

- If you lose your job or have a serious financial emergency during the 5 years of a car loan, you risk ruining your credit or even repossession if you can't make a payment. In my scenario, you can simply stop putting money away until the emergency passes and pick right back up once it is over. It might delay your purchase by a few months, you may even have to start over depending on how big the emergency is, but at least you have a car you own and you won't have the stress of collection calls.

- You get to drive a different, better car every year. When you buy a new car, you are stuck with it for at least 3 years in order to sell it to break even and get out of your loan. What if you pick a car you don't like? What if technology changes and now you want something else? My formula gives you the opportunity to try different makes and models until you find the one you really like.

And then last but definitely not least is the wonderful feeling of not being in debt. The reason the young lady at my workshop wished she had met me two years earlier is because she was under constant stress because she owed so many people so much money. When you pay cash, you are in control. The money you are putting aside is yours and you can change path anytime you want. You are not a slave to the lender. You are the banker in charge.

Cash is a beautiful thing. It gives you a little security. It brings peace because you are in control. It brings peace because you never have to worry about deadlines or phone calls. Cash is also a great bargaining tool. Odds are you will be able to take your $16,400 and buy a $20,000 car because you are laying down cash. And it is not too late for you. If you have a car loan now, work on paying it off as quickly as possible and keep your car for a while. In the meantime, use my "secret" formula to be ready to pay cash for your next car when the time comes. Paying cash for a new car – or any car – can be done and can be done by you. It is not just a wealthy person's game. Get in the game!

Toys Are Us

"I want to buy a boat, but I am not sure that I can afford it. I think I can, but I would love some guidance on how to determine if I can or not."

Suze Orman had a segment in her show entitled "Can I Afford It?". The segment consisted of people calling in with their wants and her looking at their financial snapshot and determining if they could afford it or not (really afford it). Suze looked at more than just a monthly payment. She looked at the total cost in proportion to their net worth and their current liabilities. And more times than not, they couldn't afford it.

One of the reasons is what we talked about in the last chapter – monthly payment versus overall cost. Maybe you can squeeze the monthly payment out of your current income for now, but this doesn't mean that you can truly afford the item and that the item will not disrupt your financial progress.

When I was asked the question above, obviously I needed more information from the person. I am not against toys (boats, new cars, motorcycles, etc.), but you need to make sure that you can purchase them in a way that is not going to even put one hitch in your financial journey. In this gentleman's case, he had $40,000 in retirement, he made $50,000 a year and he had $20,000 in debt.

What do you think my answer was? If you said no, you were

right. However, it didn't mean he could never have the boat; just that now is not a great time. The first step to him reaching his goal of buying the boat is obvious – he needed to get out of debt. As long as he had liabilities, he was not in a position to buy anything new, especially a depreciating toy.

This gentleman was 34 so I didn't have a lot of worries regarding his retirement. However, he needed to up his game a little in that area in order to be in a good position when the time comes. The biggest thing for me is how much money he was going to have tied up in depreciating items. My guideline is you should have no more than 30% of your yearly salary tied up in depreciating items. So for this gentleman, he should have no more than $15,000 worth of toys – and I do include cars in this even though people see them as necessities and not toys. And of course, the last criteria is paying with cash. You simply do not want to keep digging your trench deeper and deeper.

After I had all my facts from this lovely gentleman, I channeled my inner Suze and answered his ultimate question – "Can I Afford It?". He could not afford it in that moment. However, once he paid off his debt and saved up the money, he could afford it as long as the value of all his toys – in this case his car and boat – did not total more than $15,000. And of course, I recommended he step up his retirement game some, but that was just some free advice I threw in.

Toys are fun and no one loves them more than me. My dream and current goal is to own a lake house so of course, that includes a boat. However, you never want to buy anything, whether it costs $40 or $4,000, that is going to prevent you from moving forward in your financial journey or in many cases, take you backwards. And you don't want to have too much of your money tied up in depreciating assets – assets that with every use go down in value. A little bit is okay, but you want to make sure most of your money is tied up in things that are going to make you money. This is how you build wealth and stop being a broke person.

Is Leasing Ever Okay?

"Is leasing a car ever a good option?"

Recently, I was having an intense conversation with my 19-year-old daughter about all of the options for buying a car. In her mind the only option is paying cash for a used car and at her age that is the best option. No one in college or even a young adult starting a family should have a new car with an average car payment of $479 as we saw several chapters ago. But one of the many things that I have realized over my 15-year career is that there are 2 important steps in making all financial decisions: always do the math and do what will work for you personally and not anyone else.

Having said that keep in mind that debt doesn't work for anyone. Never buy anything that you do not have the money for. This is why the only option, in my book, for a millennial is paying cash for a used car. But as we get older, many of us build up our savings accounts and we end up having the money to comfortably drive a new car. So how do we decide what to do between the two options that are available for getting a new car.

The math when it comes to buying vs. leasing has to be looked at long term. For example, if you are planning on owning a car for 10 years, you need to total in the amount you pay for the car in addition to repair bills that will be paid over the course of that time. About 3 years ago, my husband and I were in need of a different vehicle. We had the financial ability to get a new car and so we began the numbers game. The van we had that needed to be replaced had 420,000 miles on it and we had owned it for 9 years. We paid $20,000 for it and had put in at least $5-6K in repairs including a new engine. That means that over the time of owning the car, it had cost us $240 a month to have that vehicle. So, we decided to look at both of our options and decide if we wanted to buy or lease our new vehicle.

I want to be up front before I go any further. Leasing is not for everyone and you should never lease just for the low payments. It can be very attractive especially to people who live in a monthly payment, paycheck to paycheck world. And just like deciding whether to rent or to buy a home, you need to do what is going to work for you in a positive way. Leasing is not what it was 20 years ago and there are advantages to leasing, but you must do your research and be honest with yourself about your needs.

Here are a few things to consider when making the decision between buying and leasing:

- When you buy a car, you own it but cars are not investments and they are only an asset to the extent of what they are worth minus what you owe. Don't pay more for a car just because you will "own" it. Research the car you are looking at and know how well they hold their value. For example, a Honda will be worth more 10 years from now than a Kia will.

- When you lease a car, you have no maintenance and this can be a big deal to many people especially as we get older. An average lease is for 36 months and that is the minimum warranty on most vehicles. And tires and brakes usually last at least 40,000 miles so you would only be responsible for oil changes which many dealerships will throw in.

- As you probably know, new cars lose value quickly in the first year or two. Most leases come with GAP insurance included which will cover the difference should your car become totaled from an accident. This is an additional purchase when buying (if you are financing) and should be included in the math.

- When you buy a car, you can drive it as many miles as you want. However, with a lease you are limited in how many miles you can drive per year (average is 12,000/year or 36,000 total). When your lease ends, if you don't purchase the vehicle you will be responsible for paying for the miles over at the rate of the lease agreement (usually .20/mile)

I am not one of those money people who says "never buy a new car" or "never lease a car". I have done the research and there are advantages to both. You can have anything but not everything. This means that in life we have to choose what is important to us and use our financial resources to do those things. A godly life has great balance. That may mean that if you have a new car you can't travel as much or have as big of a house as some. It may mean that you don't buy "stuff" everyday. But if having a nice car is important to you, you will be willing to sacrifice in other areas in order to have what adds value to your life.

Let me close with this - new cars are not evil. They are awesome and frankly can give you peace of mind when traveling the highways and byways. But they can also cripple you and take you into bankruptcy if you buy them before you have the ability to pay for them. Debt is never okay. This is true for a used car or a new car. Anytime you are looking at getting a new car, weigh all of your options, know your true financial situation and always do the math. Do what is going to move you forward, not backwards.

Home Buying – Financially Speaking

"My husband and I are ready to buy our first home. The market is great right now and we think it is the right time. We are tired of throwing away money renting. We have 3% down and a starter emergency fund of $1000. The bank has approved us for a $300,000 mortgage and we make $75,000 a year. Is this a good move to make?"

A very large percent of the US population dreams of owning a home. And many of those people consider themselves unsuccessful financially if they don't own a home. But owning a home is not a measure of success and the size of home is not a symbol of status. When you are making the decision to leap into home ownership, you must look at your financial snapshot to see if now is the time and if it isn't, lay out a plan to get there. Before I lay out the financial guidelines for buying a home, let me just say up front that there is no shame in renting. We will talk about that in a couple of chapters from now, but renting is not a negative thing. People may judge you for it, but that is their issue. Buying a home before you are financially and emotionally ready is just going to bring your grief and the home will be a burden instead of being a blessing.

So, strictly financially speaking, there are basic guidelines to follow to make sure that your new home is a blessing. Here we go:

- You must be out of debt and have at least a six-month emergency fund in place. The debt part is obvious. You don't want to take on such a large purchase when you have a bunch of little messes that need to be cleaned up. And as for the emergency fund, even if you buy a new house with a warranty, something can (and probably will) need attention and you need to make sure you have the cash funds in place to be able to take care of it. You want something going wrong to be an inconvenience not a disaster.

- You need a down payment of at least 20%. I know that it is easy to get mortgages with very little money down, but there are a couple of reasons you don't want to do that. One is you will have to carry PMI insurance until your house is at 20% equity. If you put down that 20% at purchase, you are good to go. If not, you will have an extra payment of $150-200 or more per month to cover the PMI and you will have to carry it until the bank says you are at 20% equity. Another reason is it gives you a big cushion in case the value goes down – even for just a short time. If all you put down is 3% and the market goes down, you could find yourself upside down very quickly.

- Your payment should be no more than 25-27% of your take home pay including taxes and insurance. This is a guideline that makes the house a decent percentage of your income. If you go higher than that, you are going to put a strain on other areas such as food, clothing, transportation and end up with no fun money at all. You want to make sure your payment is something that you can continue to cover in case of a job loss or medical emergency. The higher the percentage, the more trouble you will have doing this. And this is my add on – I would do 25-27% of one salary. This will keep you in a very comfortable place if someone loses a job or if they decide to stay home or start a new business. You don't want your financial commitments to get in the way of your dreams.

- You want to get a 15 year fixed rate mortgage. You want your home to become an asset at some point and the quicker you pay it off, the quicker it will add to your net worth. It is just a few dollars more a month, but it is 15 years of less interest payments so the house will cost you less in the long run. And of course, you want fixed to avoid the debacle of 2008. You want your rate to be constant and you don't want the bank to be able to make it whatever they choose on any given day.

So based on these guidelines, let's look at our question and see if this couple is ready to buy a home. Right away they aren't because they only have 3% down. Of all of the guidelines, this is probably the only one I would not say no on; however, they miss the mark on others as well. $1000 is a great starter emergency fund, but there is no way it will cover house emergencies. Remember, we are talking about expensive things when it comes to items in a home. Even a new water heater is $500. They really need at least 6 months before buying. And finally, the monthly payment is 57% of their take home pay. I don't think I need to say more on that one.

I want everyone who wants a house to have a house. But it is imperative that don't buy until you are financially ready. I hope you can see in our sample question how this couple is clearly not ready to buy right now. If they focus, in a few years they will be ready and when they are, the house they choose will be a blessing and not a burden. Don't rush the process. If you do and if you buy before being financially ready, you are going to wish you were back in your apartment, but you are going to be stuck. Be patient. I promise – it will be worth the wait.

Paying Off Your Mortgage

To many of you, this may seem impossible, but it is possible and also a very good idea.

"We have paid off all of our debt and we have a 7-month emergency fund. The only debt we have left is our mortgage. We want to pay it off, but we keep getting advice to keep it. Which is best?"

Sometimes in our finances as in life we focus on the wrong thing and we can focus so long on it that it becomes distorted. That is the case many times with paying off our mortgages. We get so caught up in the tax write offs and other things that we don't do the math and look at what is best.

A mortgage is a debt – plain and simple. The only difference is it has an asset attached to it. If it is a positive asset, you would be able to sell it if necessary to pay off the debt. However, you still have a financial obligation every month to the bank. Therefore, even if you have a positive net worth even with your mortgage, you would want to pay off your mortgage in order to get rid of your monthly obligation. This would bring you to absolute debt free status and put you on a path to wealth and financial freedom. You will also save a ton of money on the interest if you pay it off early.

Let's take a look at the biggest reasons so many people advise to keep your mortgage and see why this isn't the best advice.

- **Tax Write Off** – Right now there is a tax write off for the interest that you pay on your mortgage every year. This write off is only for people who itemize so this may eliminate you right away. However, if you do itemize, let's look at what the math is. Let's say your interest is $10,000. You would basically be paying $10,000 to keep from paying $2,500. What do I mean? Well, the interest amount is a deduction not a credit. This means that it lowers your taxable income not your tax due. If you are in a 25% tax bracket, which is the most popular, without the deduction you would owe $2,500 more in taxes. It is great to have the deduction help while you are paying down the mortgage, but as you can see the math doesn't support holding a mortgage just for the deduction.

- **More Money to Invest** – Let's say right now you are investing $300 a month. Over 30 years, that would net you $650,000. But let's say you pay off your mortgage. You now have $1500 to invest. Over the same span, this will net you $3.3 million. Wow! That's a big difference. Again, it's all about making interest, not paying interest.

Look, I get it. Mortgages are another debt that our society just assumes you will always have, but that is simply not true. At least once a day, I read a success story where a couple or even an individual either paid off their house early or they paid cash for a house. I know it sounds crazy, but it is true. It can be done.

Maybe you don't see how or maybe you don't have a lot of extra money right now. Did you know this? One extra principal payment per year can take a 30-year mortgage down to 22 ½ years and can take a 15-year mortgage down to 8 years. One extra payment – any of us can do that. And imagine if you did 2 or 3. As long as you put it all toward the principal, you will see your balance reduced significantly in a short period of time. There are really no good reasons to hold onto your mortgage payment like a pet. Set a goal to aggressively pay it off and let that money become wealth for you instead of an obligation.

A Little Behind

"My husband lost his job a couple of months ago and we have fallen behind on our mortgage. Is there anything we can do to avoid this ruining our credit or us losing our house?"

I always feel a little sad when I get emails and questions like this one. I'm not sad because someone lost their job – that can be a huge opportunity for them to go and do something bigger and better. I'm sad because this means that they didn't have an emergency fund in place as an umbrella for when the storm hit.

But I digress. Unfortunately, this happens more times than not any time an emergency hits. And frankly, sometimes it happens when everything is going good. If you are not financially ready to buy a home like we covered a few chapters ago, or you simply buy more home than you can afford, you can find yourself in this position even without a major life change such as a job loss or a medical emergency. 75% of Americans live paycheck to paycheck – this is all Americans, no matter what their income is. This is really sad.

But I digress again. Anytime you do a budget, whether it is just your regular every month budget or it is a budget during a crisis, you need to put your expenses in order of importance. You never want to pay a credit card bill before your mortgage – never. The items that get paid first always are utilities, housing, food, and transportation. These are things that you need to keep you and your family going. Many people put clothes on this list, but I am willing to bet you have plenty of clothes to carry you through the emergency. Yes, clothes are a necessity, but not a priority.

When you get behind on any of your bills, communication is key. If you are in communication with the companies involved, most of them will work with you in order to keep your account current and your credit in good standing. If you don't communicate and just sit back and let the chips fall where they may, they will be less likely to work with you as time goes by.

When you find yourself in this position, I would also like to encourage you to try not to develop a victim mentality. You don't want to sit around wallowing in your problems. You want to be a problem solver and find solutions to your dilemmas.

Anytime you find yourself slipping behind on any bill, take a good hard look at your budget. You need to slash as many things as you can until you get everything caught up. You may have to not eat out, cut out your lattes, eat soup and sandwiches, or cut back on other things. Sometimes life requires a short sacrifice for a great gain. Cutting back on some of your bills will prevent you from mounting up late fees and extra interest that falling behind can cause.

One more thing – if you find that your situation is a little more permanent than you first thought, be proactive. It is not what anyone wants, but you may need to sell your house and downsize or even rent until the crisis passes. What you want to do is make sure that you maintain control of the situation. You don't want to look up one day and see a notice from the sheriff that the bank is foreclosing on you. If you know you are out of options, take immediate steps to sell your home yourself. Doing so will prevent you from having a foreclosure on your credit and will keep the control of the sale in your hands. If a bank gets ahold of it, they will sell it for much less than you can and you will end up owing the difference.

Sometimes, we all make bad choices and get in over our heads. And sometimes life happens and we don't have an umbrella to keep us from getting wet. But know matter what position you find yourself in, keep a positive attitude, look at all your options, be willing to make small sacrifices for big gain, and keep control as long as you can. You are the author of your own story! Don't give your pen to anyone else!

Renting versus Buying

Before I get to the specific question, I want to just say one thing. Society has put status symbols out there that are a myth. How successful you are financially is not based on how big your house is, how much you spent on it, or whether you own a home or rent. These are society based expectations and are not real. As a matter of fact, many very successful people, in the area of their finances, rented until they could pay cash for a small home and then upgraded only to the point where they were content. A great lesson I learned in my journey was you have to live your authentic life – no one else's. What works for you and what makes you happy is going to be completely different than what makes me happy and that is okay. I am going to make choices in how I spend my money that are going to be completely different than you. Maybe I would love to travel right now – which I do love to travel. Well, in order to do that, I may need to rent for awhile and that is perfectly okay. Personal finance is personal and you should never – I repeat never – compare yourself or your finances to anyone else's, even a family member like a parent or sibling. You are you – and you need to do whatever works for you and you alone. Now let me get off my soapbox and get to the question.

"We are saving up to buy a house and we are currently renting. We don't quite have the money to buy yet, but everyone keeps telling us we are just throwing our money away by renting. What should we do?"

The obvious answer at this point after reading the last few chapters is to keep renting until you are financially ready to buy a house. I don't need to go over that again. But I will address the common mantra when it comes to this subject – "You are just throwing money away." And this isn't necessarily true. Let's lay out two completely different scenarios and see if you can tell the difference:

- A couple is renting a two-bedroom apartment for $800 a month. They make $75,000 a year and they have no debt. They also have around $20,000 in savings and $70,000 in a retirement account.

- A couple owns a house. The house is worth $200,000 and they owe $170,000 on it. They make $100,000 a year and have $25,000 in debt not including the house. They have $10,000 in savings and $40,000 in retirement.

Which couple is better off? Many of you would say the couple who owns the house is, but odds are your answer is strictly based on the fact that they own a home. But the reality is the first couple is in better shape in this moment.

Let's look at it strictly from a net worth standpoint. Yes, the second couple owns a nice home, but financially they are worse off than the first couple. The net worth of couple one is $90,000. The net worth of couple two is $55,000. So one thing we can see is that owning a home doesn't always put you in a better financial state. By renting, the first couple has been able to save more and invest more because they don't have the added expenses that come with home ownership (repairs, taxes, etc.) and they chose a size that works for them. Just like transportation, we all have a shelter expense

– it is a necessity – but how much it is should be dependent on our income, our budget and our future goals. The second couple decided to invest in a home where the first couple decided to invest in mutual funds. Neither one is "throwing their money away."

When I started my journey 20 years ago, I started by renting a room from a lady in her basement. A few months later, I moved up to a studio apartment. Then a one bedroom and eventually a 4-bedroom house. You do what you need to do and what works best for you no matter what anyone thinks. I know people who rent their entire lives because it is what worked for them and their dreams. Some people rent forever simply because they don't want to deal with repairs and the costs associated with owning.

Whatever the reason, know this – whatever you decide to do is okay as long as it works for your situation and moves your forward in your finances and in your life. Please do not make decisions based on other people's judgments of your situation – a situation they know nothing about. If you need or want to rent, there is no shame. My grandparents had to sell their property once in order to deal with some medical issues. They ended up renting for a long time after. But they did what they needed to do and they had their priorities in order and I can promise you, they did not care what other people thought.

Renting in and of itself is not "throwing money away". However, what you do with the money you save may fall under that category. But again, that is all about personal choices – personal finance is personal.

Mortgage Refinancing

"We got our mortgage 7 years ago at a higher rate – 6%. We have worked on our credit and paid down our mortgage and we now qualify for a refinance at 4%. Is this worth it and are there any risks in refinancing our mortgage?"

There are many reasons to consider refinancing your home and the one in the question above is just one of them. It is always enticing to think about the lower monthly payment that a refinance will bring, but you want to make sure that the refinance isn't going to end up costing you money.

The one thing this client left out of the original question was how much the fees are to do the refinance. There are fees and closing costs associated with most refinances and you need to know the cost before making this decision. It is not as black and white as saving 2% in interest.

You need to analyze your break even point – the point where your savings per year cover the cost of the refinance. For example, if your cost to refinance is $2,000, how long until you recover those costs? Let's say that refinancing saves you $100 a month. Then 20 months is your break even. The next thing to look at is are you planning on staying in the home long enough to cover your break even – in our example, 20 months. If you are, then it is worth it. If you are not, then it isn't. The point here is that if you sell the house before your break even, odds are you are going to lose money and that is never our goal. You just want to make sure it is a wise decision for the long haul and not just about the 2%.

If you do decide to refinance, make sure you ask for a par quote or a zero quote. This means that the closing costs will not include points or origination fees. You never want to pay these fees as they are simply pre-paid interest. It may look like you are saving money, but if you do the math, odds are you are not.

I want to make sure I add that if you have an ARM (Adjustable Rate Mortgage), you want to refinance that to a fixed rate as soon as you can. The break even on an ARM is impossible to figure out so you want to refinance no matter what in this scenario. You want to make sure that your rate is a fixed rate so that your payment stays steady throughout the loan.

If you are refinancing in order to go to a lower interest rate or to get out of a variable loan, that is awesome and in most cases, is the way to go. However, if you are refinancing simply to go from a 30-year loan to a 15-year loan, refinancing is not necessary. You can just take your balance and run it through a mortgage calculator, find out what your payment would be on a 15 year and make that payment every month – making sure that the extra is going to the principal only.

Refinancing is a great tool to use in order to save money on your loan (mortgages and auto loans as well). Especially if your finances are in a much better place than they were when you took out the loan. But just like everything else, you want to take the time to make sure it is a good choice for you and is actually going to save you money. If it is, go for it. It is all about moving forward.

Getting More Bang For Your Buck

"We have worked really hard and we are now financially ready to buy a house. The bank says we can finance $325,000, but I don't feel comfortable with that much. Using the 25% guideline, we can do about $210,000. I do have certain things I would like to have. How do we find the best house and the best price?"

First of all, I want to address the awesome realization of this client that they did not have to accept every dollar that the bank approved. The bank will almost always approve you for way more than the 25% guideline and it is up to you to figure out what you can truly afford. Simply use any mortgage calculator and using 25% of your take home pay, work backwards to get your maximum loan amount.

Whether that amount is $80,000 or $210,000 like in our question, you want to get the most home for that amount. And the best home available to you at that price. You want to make sure going in that you focus on the three L's – location, layout and lot and not the three C's – color, cleanliness and condition. All of these are important. However, the three C's can be changed and improved – the three L's cannot. So you want to focus first on the things you can't change. For example, if you really want to live in a ranch home, buying a 2 story home is going to make you unhappy. You cannot change the layout; however, you can change appliances, wall color, etc.

I used to watch the house hunting shows on television and I would cringe every time someone would go through the list of what they wanted. It wasn't that they had a list of wants – it was that they focused on things they could change and not on things they couldn't. And almost every time they would say "I have to have ...". Granite countertops are not a need. You need to be realistic. We all want new everything – granite countertops, stainless steel appliances, hardwood floors, remodeled bathrooms – but these things may not be in your budget right now. And if they are, they may come in a smaller home. You have to have priorities and you have to figure out what you can live with and what you can't before you even start.

If you are a first time homebuyer, odds are you are going to have to make lots of sacrifices at first to find a home in your budget. Just remember – you can make improvements as you go along. I still have white laminate countertops in my kitchen that have been there for over 18 years. They are not fancy, but countertops are not more important to me than other things. One day I will probably replace them, but right now, other things take priority. It is much easier to make improvements than it is to downsize which is a possibility if you bite off more than you can chew.

When you walk into a home, consider everything. Do you like where the home is located? Do you like the layout and do you like the lot it sits on? If the answer is yes, then keep it on the list. However, if the only reason you are saying no to a great home is the color of the walls or the fact that it has carpet instead of hardwoods, you need to keep in mind that those things can be changed over time. And if you have to have them, you simply can't live without them, then you may have to consider a different location or layout. It is very challenging to find the perfect house – perfect in every way, but know that you can make any house into the home you want over time.

My parents moved into their second home 45 years ago. When they bought it, it was a simple 3-bedroom ranch in a great neighbor. And over the next 43 years, my mom and dad made improvements to it to turn it into their dream home. They redid the bathroom, built on a den addition, built on a 3 level screened in porch, got new carpet several times, and after 35 years, my mom finally got a new kitchen. They bought what they could afford, paid off a 20-year mortgage in 10 years and spent the next 33 years improving it and building their dream home.

We live in an instant society nowadays. We think that everything has to be perfect immediately. But I love the example my parents set for me that you can have everything you ever dream of over the course of time. It is true that home is where the heart is. We were happy in the small 3-bedroom ranch and we were happy in the dream home as well. It is nice to have a home that you love - just make sure you do it in a way that works for you and your family. Your dream home is out there waiting for you, but it may mean you have to build it over time.

Getting On The Same Page

"I desperately want to get out of debt; however, my husband is not on board. He is the spender and I am the saver; therefore, we are looking at our finances in different ways. How to I get him to agree with me when it comes to getting out of debt?"

The issue here is not one of getting out of debt or not. This is an issue about being on the same page and this issue can pop up in any and all areas of a relationship. When I do premarriage counseling, I work with couples to make sure that they are on the same page in four areas of life: kids, money, religion and family (siblings, in-laws, etc.).

Let me clarify what I mean by being on the same page. It doesn't necessarily mean that you are in 100% agreement, but it does mean that you are working together to come to a positive solution. In most areas, it is a positive thing to have a balance of two different ways. In this example, it is great that one is a spender and one is a saver. If you have two of either one, it can make for a very unbalanced scenario. However, balance comes from a give and take and a mutual understanding and compromise.

Based on the way this question is worded, this lady and her husband are on completely different sides and both have dug their heels in when it comes to their position. She really wants to pay off their debt and I would imagine he is not a fan of the budget or the sacrifices that will need to be made for a short time. I deduce this simply from the fact that she said he is the spender and it seems that he is refusing to even contemplate the possibility of getting out of debt.

When it comes to finances in a marriage, each person needs to have a voice and there should be a mutual agreement and understanding in all areas. For example, if the husband is afraid of losing something or not being able to spend, the wife can assure him that they can try to work certain things into the budget at the same time they are getting out of debt. And instead of her going full on, maybe they ease into the process. But the husband needs to understand that the debt is styming their future dreams and the quicker they pay it off, the quicker they can begin to build wealth and spend more.

You never want to come at each other with loud voices and strong opinions. When you are having the conversations, you should do it in a quiet, loving way. This is the best way to get your voice heard – and that goes for both sides. Setting aside a date night for this is an awesome solution – a little wine, some candles, some Italian food – this sets the mood for a calm conversation which will lead to perfect solutions.

Again, this is an issue you want to address before you get married so there is clear communication protocol in all situations and no one is blindsided by someone's feelings especially on the big four that I mentioned. If you are already married and you didn't take this step, don't worry. It is not too late. It may take time and maybe even a third party, but I truly believe you can get on the same page on these issues as well.

Make sure that as you are addressing your wants and concerns, that you do it in a clear and concise way, never blaming the other person. And make sure that the other person feels that they can do the same. The most important thing is that you are on the same page and have some sort of agreement and understanding. I would never recommend this, but even if you both agree to be in debt forever, at least you are on the same page. That is better then being on two different pages. You will actually make more progress being on the same page than you will if you are not.

For a large part of my life, I always wanted to get my way. And I believe on some level we all do. But I finally learned that life – especially marriage – is about give and take. If one person is always winning, then no one is really winning. It has become easier for me over the years to not always get my way. Don't misunderstand – for a minute, I am disappointed, but it is easier for me to move on and not have to always get exactly what I want. First things first – make sure each voice is heard and secondly, work on a situation until you can come to a compromise you can both agree on. It's in there – sometimes you just have to dig it out.

Financial Infidelity

"I just found out that my wife has been hiding purchases she has made for years and when I asked about it, she said it was my fault because we never have any money to splurge. I even found out she opened a credit card in my name without me knowing. I don't know if I can ever trust her again. Is there any advice you can give me to help us get back to a good place?"

This is actually a very common problem especially today when access to credit and things is so easy. Let me start out by saying that there is probably a much deeper issue here than what it appears to be. On the surface, it appears to be a woman who wants a bunch of "stuff" and is getting it whether they have the money or not. But odds are that isn't the root of it.

Financial infidelity starts the same way sexual infidelity or emotional infidelity start and has the same repercussions when it is discovered. Some people do not consider this a serious issue, but when a trust is broken in a marriage or relationship, it is very serious.

The first thing you have to do is seek some sort of counseling with a good therapist and one in the personal finance arena, even a coach, would be an added bonus. Since I am one of these, let me share what I would do if this couple came to me for counseling.

Many fights, heated discussions and even divorces that

occur sight money as the primary issue. However, in most cases, this isn't the case. What happens is because money is such a big part of our lives and since it is such a personal issue, this is the area where other issues will show up.

The wife in this situation has deeper issues than just a spending addiction. Like all addictions – and yes, spending addiction is a real addiction – there is something deeper that the person is not dealing with and it is manifesting itself in the addiction. I would identify this as an addiction because she felt the need to hide it. When you are confident in your decisions, there is no need to hide them. Therefore, I would want to work with the wife and find out what the deeper issue is.

The husband in this situation shares some of the burden of the problem. They always say never to blame the victim and in this case, it looks like he is the victim. However, he obviously wasn't involved in the finances or he would have noticed something sooner. There is no excuse for the actions of the wife, but there is also no excuse for the husband to be that out of touch in the area of their finances. We would also do a check in to address why the wife felt the need to hide everything and make sure that there is not a controlling or judgment issue there. My ex husband didn't get mad when I bought something, but he was constantly belittling what I bought. I got to the point where I would just hide all my purchases from him simply because I didn't want to hear the belittling.

Now let's be clear. Just like with other types of infidelity, both parties carry some of the burden. If you had a great relationship with lots of love and understanding, no one would ever feel the need to stray or hide anything. Infidelity of any kind is never okay, but we must be honest about it in order to rebuild and have it never happen again.

He asked me what could he do to build the trust back up and get back to a good place. Anytime he is talking with her about this issue, whether with a therapist or at home (and even in future discussions), he must use a loving tone. Attacking her is just going to keep her there and nothing will ever heal. He also needs to look really deep into himself and identify the role he played – whether it was checking out of the finances, being controlling, belittling – whatever role he played he must identify and correct. And I belief that if he would apologize for his part and be willing to listen, odds are she would open up more about why she did it. This will bring about understanding, clarification, and eventually healing.

If financial infidelity has happened in a marriage or relationship, it can't be swept under the rug. It must be addressed as soon as it is discovered if not before. I highly recommend working with a professional and not trying to heal this on your own. There is always a reason the person did it and even if you think it's not valid, it is to them and needs to be addressed before the marriage can heal. Remember that the infidelity is just an action for a much deeper issue. Once you go all the way to the root, you can begin to heal it and the healing will spread all the way to the surface.

The Business of Divorce

52% of marriages end in divorce and 80% of those site financial problems as the reason. As we saw in the last chapter, the problems are usually much deeper than money, but this is where they will rear their ugly heads because it is such a sensitive and personal issue. Before we proceed with the question, I feel like I must make a public service announcement – if you are considering divorce for any reason (financial, adultery, no more love, etc.), please seek counseling before throwing in the towel. Many times the issues can be dealt with and worked through with the help of a third party. Please don't give up before giving it every chance you can. Now back to our regularly scheduled program.

"My wife and I are getting a divorce and I am unclear on what the financial obligations are when it comes to bank accounts, credit cards, home and auto loans, retirement, and more. Any guidance would be appreciated."

Before I go too far, let me just say that each state has its own rules for many things and you will definitely want to consult a lawyer regarding the details. However, I am happy to share things that are pretty consistent from a financial standpoint.

Let's address debt first as that is the most consistent. It's actual pretty simple. If a debt has your name on it, you are legally responsible in the eyes of the lender no matter what a judge says. For example, if you have a credit card with both of your names on it and the judge says she is responsible for it, in the eyes of the lender you both still are. If she doesn't pay, the lender will expect you to pay and the payment history or anything else associated with this card will report to your credit report. If a judge issues a court order regarding the debt, you may be able to use it to have your name removed from the debt. This will be at the discretion of the lender, but I have had great success with this. Just make sure that you understand a court order by a judge, believe it or not, is not enough to get you out of being responsible for the debt. You will need to follow up with the lender. And again, don't be surprised if they won't remove you. If they don't, I personally would work on paying the debt off because if you leave it to the other person, they can ruin your credit very quickly. Divorce turns a marriage into a business transaction and many times one party is out to ruin the other party since during this time emotions are running high. Make sure to protect yourself – legally and emotionally.

When it comes to assets in a marriage, these are usually divided up as the judge sees fit. You will want to make sure that if you are awarded an asset that you do what you need to do to legally change the paperwork. For example, if you are awarded the house, make sure that you legally remove the other person's name from it. This protects you and them as they are liable if anything happens as long as their name is on it. If you are ordered to split an asset you have two options usually: to sell the item and split the profit or one person buys the other person out. In our house example, if you were ordered to split it, you would either have to sell it, pay off all debt connected to it, and split the profit or the other option would be for whoever wants to live there to buy out the other person. For example, if the equity is $50,000, then they would need to give the other party $25,000 in order to keep it. See what I mean about a business transaction.

Items such as child and spousal support are determined by each state and in many cases each county. For example, in Pennsylvania where I live, each county has a formula for both and there is no negotiating. It is determined strictly on income and how long you have been married. Many states are going to this formula based system as it is very straightforward; however, you definitely want to check with your lawyer on how it is determined in your state.

Divorce is a horrible thing and should be avoided at all costs. But many times it can't. I see so many couples who really never should have married in the first place and this seems to be more and more. If you are single, please take your time and find the right person for you. It will save you a lot of time and heartache. I would rather wait for someone who is perfect for me than to ever go through a divorce again. I've been through one and it is no picnic. There are not perfect people out there, but there are people who are a great fit for you and you for them. Keep looking until you find them. You won't regret it. If you are married, do everything you can to find the love and joy everyday. And don't be afraid to seek counseling if you need it. Sometimes we just aren't sure how to deal with something or someone and there is no shame in going to a qualified third party and seeking answers and learning. Many couples have come through my office (literally and through Skype) and I am proud to say most of their marriages have only grown from the experience. This isn't always the case, but you have to at least try.

Let me just say one more time – divorce turns marriage into a business transaction. If you find yourself in this position, protect yourself and seek great legal counsel throughout the process. It is what is best for all parties involved.

Kids and Money

"We have 3 kids, ages 6, 4 and 2. When is a good time to start teaching them about money and what do you teach them? There is so much to know and we are not sure where to start."

This is a great question. I always get excited with this one because it means that a parent is aware of their finances and wants to teach their kids about money as well. I learned very little about money growing up. It was a very taboo subject for many reasons – mostly due to a privacy issue. I was told what to do – basically save for what you need and want, but I wasn't really taught with specific examples. My parents were a great overall example – I just had no clue how they did it. This is why I get so excited to teach kids and teens all about money and personal finance.

The first thing you need to do is make sure whatever you teach is age appropriate. You aren't going to teach your 6-year-old how to invest. But you can teach every kid the 4 aspects of money anytime, at any age – work, give, save and spend. We will go into greater detail in the next chapter, but no child is too young to learn this.

You heard me say many times already – personal finance is personal and this applies to kids as well. You want to make sure you are teaching your kids in a personal way and in a way that works for them. Everyone learns different and this applies to children as well as adults. This may mean that what you do for one child may not work for another, but the overall concepts are pretty consistent.

If you look really close, you will find teachable moments everywhere. And you can teach your kids without giving out personal information – as was my parents fear. Children don't have a filter to know when something is private so it is a valid concern; however, don't miss out on teaching them valuable lessons because of this. Find a way to make your point even if you just make up the numbers. For example, you don't have to say "We make $100,000 a year." You can just use made up numbers to make a point. Let's say you are teaching them about saving – you want them to learn to save at least 10%. You don't have to tell them how much that is for you – just say, "If you make $100, then you need to set aside $10 for savings." You are teaching them concepts; therefore, being specific using your finances isn't necessary. Don't feel obligated to tell them and don't miss a teachable moment because of it. Your detailed finances should be private; your lessons should not.

And please never be ashamed to admit mistakes you have made or are making. Let your mistakes become teachable moments as well. My daughter knew about my journey every step of the way. In general terms at first, but when she turned 16 and got a job, I was a little more specific. And at 19, she is making awesome financial decisions. Not because it came naturally to her, but because she has learned from me – my knowledge and my mistakes. Now, of course, I may be an exception since my story has been told worldwide, but my point is don't be ashamed. Be proud of how far you have come, what you have learned, and pass those lessons down to your children so they don't make the same mistakes.

Anytime the subject of money is discussed, you want to make sure that you are discussing it in a way that is balanced. Money is not the answer to everything. It is necessary to buy our needs and our wants, but it should never be an obsession and take over our lives. We need to make sure we keep money in it's rightful place.

Money is a very important subject that needs to be covered with your children. But like all other important subjects – sex, drugs, drinking, etc. – you always want it to be age appropriate. And I want to say again – consider being honest and sharing your experiences with your children. If me sharing my mistakes can keep my daughter from making one, it is worth it. Teach your children – don't just tell them.

4 Aspects of Money

"What are the most important things we should teach our children when it comes to money? We aren't really sure where to start."

Another parent loving their children enough to teach them about money and personal finance – I love it!

There are four aspects of money that everyone needs to know, child and adult alike: work, give, save and spend – and in that order. Let's talk about it.

You have to work in order to have any money. It is hard for children to grasp this because so much is just handed to them. It is imperative that they learn that hard work equals money. Giving is a vital part of the formula. If we keep every dollar we make and spend it on ourselves, then we become selfish people. Selfish people don't build wealth. Saving is important because you never know where life is going to take you and you need an umbrella when it rains. And of course, spending is a part because we all need to have a little fun. Let's look at each one in a little more detail so that you will know what it is that your children (and you) need to learn.

- **Work –** Working is not the only way to get money, but it is the best way. The only other way is to have it handed to you and that is not good from any angle. Working hard brings about a sense of pride and accomplishment. You can't get that from having money just handed to you. When you work for the money, you respect it more. It brings a bigger value than just the numbers on the paycheck. And I would also encourage your children to do the work that they are passionate about. Do what you love and the money will follow. This is a very true saying. No matter what age your children are they can begin to work for their money. My daughter, from the age of 6, worked for her fun money. There were things she did just because she lived here – things like making her bed, cleaning her room, and helping in the kitchen. But there were also things that she could do to earn money such as vacuum, help in the yard, etc. Teach your kids to work hard and to be proud of the work they accomplish. If they get this, they will never have trouble earning the money they need.

- **Give** – Giving is a heart issue – plain and simple. You need to be able to share some of what you have with others. This can come in the form of money, but can also be shown in the form of time and stuff. Teach your kids to give the toys that they have outgrown to someone who needs them. Teach your kids to find a cause they love and give to it – time and money. This life isn't all about us and there are always people less fortunate and in need. Teach your kids to be compassionate and giving people. They are never too young to give.

- **Save** – If you don't save, you will never be prepared when you have a need. A simple rule that you can teach them is the 80-10-10 rule – give 10%, save 10% and live on 80%. If they save 10% of every dollar they make, they will always have money. You also want them to learn that every purchase isn't instant. Sometimes when we want something, we have to be patient and save for it. If they can learn this principal, they will never use debt for anything. And isn't that the best lesson ever!

- **Spend** – Yes, it is okay to spend. We can have anything, just not everything. We have to learn to take the 80% left after giving and saving and budget around it. There is a lot they can do with their 80%, but they have to learn to prioritize. They also have to learn by making bad buying decisions every so often. This is a better lesson with their money than with yours. There were a lot of things my daughter wanted. When she had to start spending her money, she learned to want less. And when she made a bad buying decision, she learned and tried not to make that mistake again.

We are raising adults. Whether your kid is 2, 12, or 22, we are raising adults and everything we teach them, they are going to take into adulthood. We need to teach them life skills that will take them in positive directions in their life. When it comes to the subject of money, teaching them these four aspects will send them well on their way to wealth and financial freedom.

College 101

The question we are talking about next is in regards to paying for college. But before I dive into the question, I want to address a bigger issue. When it comes to college and adulting, we tend to put the cart before the horse. So many high school seniors are going to college simply because they are expected to. They go, they pick a major, they graduate, and then find out they hate what they picked for a career. So before we get into how to pay for college, we need to set the record straight. College is not for everyone and if a person chooses to not go to college this does not make them "less than". As I spoke briefly about in the last chapter, we all – kids and adults alike – need to find our passion. Before anyone signs up to go to college, you need to determine what you are passionate about and in what area you want to work. You can figure this out by job shadowing, doing internships, or just hanging out with someone for a few days. My daughter eliminated 3 careers very quickly her junior and senior year by doing job shadowing and attending a week long summer camp. Once your child has figured out what they want to do, then you look at what they need to do it. If your child wants to be a cosmetologist, they don't need a four-year degree. They simply need to go to cosmetology school and hone their craft. College is simply a form of training. There are jobs that require this type of training and some that require even more training. A doctor is not going to be a doctor with just a certificate. But there is absolutely no need for a carpenter to have a masters (or undergrad for that matter). Let's put the horse back in front of the cart – help your child to determine their passion as best as they can and then determine the path they need to take to get there. And if it requires college, then we move on to the question.

"Our daughter is a senior in high school. She will be attending college in the fall. We don't have a lot saved toward her tuition. What are the best loans out there for her?"

Okay, of course you know the first comment I'm going to make – there are no good loans out there. Another myth circling our society is that the only way to attend college and get an education is to go into debt and take our loans. This is simply not the case. I know many people who pay cash for their schooling and I want to share with you how to do that.

The first step we talked about – make sure you don't take on more schooling than you need. This will save you tons of money. Now, let's assume what your child wants to do requires a four-year degree – like a teacher or engineer. Let's look at all of the different ways that you and him/her can cash flow this very large expense.

- **Community College** – Education is education. An English class from the local community college is just as good as the English class from the state college. I always recommend taking your first two years of classes from the local community college. You are going to save a whole lot of money between tuition and room & board. And again, the education is the same. You just want to make sure that the classes you are taking will transfer to the four-year college you are looking to attend. My daughter is currently attending a university in Connecticut. Because of scholarships and our contributions, she was able to go there for all four years. However, she took classes over the summer and over winter break from the local community college online and saved over $10,000 and is graduating a year early because of it, saving an additional $23,000. You want to make sure you shop all of your options and don't just sign your future away to student loans.

- **Your new job** – As a senior in high school, your child has one job – apply to every scholarship out there. If they apply for 1000, they may get 10, but that can be worth $10,000 or more. Scholarships are free money. My daughter had over half of her tuition paid for in scholarships her first year and even more as she has found more scholarships along the way. This can be a tedious process, and a little discouraging, but again even one scholarship can make a big difference.

- **Work** – Your children are not to good to work. When I was in college, I worked 40 hours a week. It can be done and I promise they won't die. This may cut into their social lives, but they are there to get an education. Socializing takes a back burner to that. But believe me, I found a way to work it in.

- **Your help** – Any cash help that you can give is great. Just make sure that you don't dip into your retirement and mess up your future to pay for it. They can get a small loan if needed, but you can't get a loan for retirement.

And after all is said and done, if they absolutely have to take out a small loan, make sure that they work on paying it off while in school and attack it quickly as soon as they graduate.

Look, I have seen way too many college graduates crying and desperate because they had no idea what the real world was going to be like. They live in this movie where they go to college, graduate and the next day start their new job making $75,000 a year. This just isn't the realty for most. And when they graduate, life starts adding other bills to the mix – rent, car, utilities, food, clothes, entertainment, etc. That can be extremely overwhelming. So many graduates put off paying their loans for months and you are simply digging a bigger hole.

Student loans are the easiest loans to get, but easy is not always better (why do you think they are so easy). Do everything you can to get as much free money as you can (scholarships, grants, etc.), work two jobs over the summer and pile up cash, and if you must take out a loan, take out the lowest possible amount and pay it back as quickly as you can. There is no time limit on getting the education you need. We have made it four years, but you can take as long as you need to do it right and in a way that will set you up for an awesome future. You have your whole life ahead of you. Don't add stress with loans before you even get going.

The Dreaded "N" Word

"My wife and I are having trouble with our kids when it comes to saying no. We want to give them what they want most of the time, but when we do tell them no, there is always screaming and fighting. Sometimes we actually give in. I know this isn't healthy for them or for us, but how to we stop the madness?"

This gentleman is correct. This is not healthy for them or for the children. We all must hear the word no sometimes, and children are no exception. Whether it is because something isn't good for them or it is just not okay right now, the word no cannot become a bad word.

I am amazed at how many adults from my generation and younger constantly say "I just want my children to have everything that I didn't." It amazes me because my parent's generation were becoming parents at a time when incomes were rising and there was more "stuff" available than ever before. But since they grew up with parents from the depression era, they still had a little bit of that in them – enough to be able to find the balance between more and too much.

However, my generation grew up with more so we have absolutely no idea what it is like to have nothing. And this just gets worse with every generation, especially with the access to credit so readily available. You can literally have everything instantly. With this mindset, we are teaching our children that all they have to do is ask for it and they get it. This is not only going to become a problem in their financial life, but it will also create issues in their relationships and careers. Can you imagine marrying someone who literally had to get exactly what they wanted or they would throw a fit?

Look – I know it is so much easier just to give a child what they want so that you don't have to hear it. But once again, the easy way is definitely not the best way. We must say no to our children when it is appropriate and not be afraid of their reactions. And here is a helpful hint – don't turn "no" into a curse word. Learn to say things like "Not right now" or "We are not going to do that" or "That is not in this month's budget". If all you do is yell "no" at them constantly, they are going to get defensive. Your tone and wording can make a world of difference.

Now, if you are like the author of our question, and you haven't said no in a really long time, it is going to take several times until it begins to stick. Remember, these are children and their minds aren't able to process everything the same as an adult. Be patient with them, but also be firm in your decision. And if you children happen to be older, it may take even more to get through. When I decided to start saying no to my daughter, I actually sat her down and told her that I had been wrong in never telling her no. That in trying to make her happy, I had actually hurt her because we all have to learn that we always can't have everything we want.

Whatever method is going to work for you, do it. Don't continue with the genie routine just because saying no might be a little uncomfortable. Realize this – whether you are 4,

14, 24 or 44, no one likes to be told no. But we must all learn to accept that sometimes this is the answer we are going to receive and we need to be okay with it. Teaching your children this at an early age is a gift to them even if they can't see it. And if your kids are older, don't just throw in the towel. It is never too late to give the gift of no.

Allowance vs. Commission

"We want to pay our kids for the chores that they do. We don't want to just hand them an allowance. We believe that they should do something for the money. What do you recommend amount wise in this area?"

As we talked about in an earlier chapter, you definitely want to make sure that there is some work associated with any money you give them. What you call it isn't really important, but I always used the word commission with my daughter and this is why.

Commission implies that you are paid based on what you do. Allowance is usually a set amount that you get whether you complete the task or not. It is important that they learn to work for it, so that is why I chose to use the word commission. It is a little easier to get them to do stuff when they are younger because the tasks aren't as difficult, but as they get older, you may need to get creative at times. I came up with a fun idea when my daughter was 12 that I would like to share. At that age, you really start to get the slacking off when it comes to tasks and my daughter was no different. So I wrote out a contract for her. It stated what was expected and what each task paid. It also stated that she would only be paid on what she did – no freebies. And then I added one more goody to the contract – if she failed to do tasks 3 times, she would be written up. And if it continued for 2 more times, she would be fired. What this meant was she would still do the work, but she would do it for free.

Believe me, when she failed to do the tasks once and realized I wasn't joking, she stepped up her game. If she had to do the tasks, she at least wanted to be paid. I did this as a lesson on how a real job works.

So many parents just hand their children a few dollars every week for just being themselves. Doing this teaches them that they do not have to work for their money and as we have already talked about, associating work to money is a key component to the process.

Another thing that I have seen recently, that wasn't around when I needed it, is a chore board with cash clipped to each chore. This is great for multiple kids because the ones who work harder make more money. If a kid doesn't like what they are making, they will need to step up their game in order to make more. I highly recommend Pinterest for this idea and many other versions of it.

Work can and should be fun. You don't want to just hand them money without work, but there is no reason why they should dread the work either. And as with everything else, make sure that the chore and the money attached is appropriate for the age of the child. You don't want to have your 5-year-old cutting grass. And you don't want your 15-year-old getting paid $20 for cutting grass. This is where social sites and blogs can come in handy for great ideas along with payment suggestions.

Every child needs to do things around the house simply because they are a part of the family and every child needs to learn the value of work and a commission system is a great way to do that. So no matter what you call it – commission or allowance – make it fun, age appropriate, and life like so that your child learns how the real world works in a safe environment first. You don't want them to be shocked when they start a job and realize that money isn't just handed to them. Remember, we are raising adults.

Life Insurance 101

"I am 23 years old and wondering if I should buy life insurance. I feel like, at my age, it isn't necessary, but I am not sure when the best time to buy it is in order to lock in a good rate. Also, I hear term is the best, but my agent says whole life is better. Any help would be appreciated."

This question has two separate issues in it – when to buy and what type – and we are going to address both. First, let's look at when. If you are 23, single, with no debt, you really don't need life insurance right now. The purpose of life insurance is simply to cover certain expenses if you don't live long enough or have the money to cover them. Another purpose of life insurance is to replace some of the income you might lose if a spouse departs early. Neither of these apply to the author of this question; therefore, my advice to him/her would be to not buy at this time as long as they are single and debt free.

However, when you are married and especially when you have children, you really need some amount of life insurance in case you depart this world earlier than anticipated. You need to make sure that your family is provided for in the future in the event of an early departure. Life insurance is there to replace your salary and to make sure that big things like mortgages and college tuition are covered. Can you live without life insurance? Sure. Is it a necessity? Not really. But I like to consider it an inexpensive gift to your loved ones in the event of your death. Would you want your spouse to struggle if you knew that $25 a month could avoid it? Of course not. That is why I always recommend life insurance to anyone with a spouse and/or children until you have the money to self insure – which we will talk about in a minute.

You are probably thinking what kind of insurance can I get for $25 a month. The best kind – term life insurance. There are two types of life insurance – whole and term – and they are the same but very different. Let's look at each one individually and you can see why.

- **Whole Life** – Whole life insurance is more expensive than term for lower coverage than term. Why is that? The big sell on a whole life policy is that you can borrow money against it. Basically, it has a savings plan within the policy. However, it really doesn't. When I think savings, I think cash that earns a little interest that is mine to keep. However, savings in a whole life policy is more like a credit line – it is an amount that they set that you can borrow if needed. But here is the big thing – when you die, the face amount of the policy is all that is paid out. There is no extra "savings" given to your loved ones. And, if you happen to have a loan against the policy, that amount will be deducted from the face value. Crazy right? And it can cost you upwards of $150 or more per month for a $100,000 policy.

- **Term Life** – Term life is simple. You get what you buy when you die. No gimmicks, no tricks. And a $500,000 policy is about $25/month or less, depending on your age and health. If you are young when you get the policy (age 25-35), you can get a half a million-dollar insurance policy for the price of a steak. The only difference with term is it has a set time limit – a term – to it. But for your $25 a month cost, you can get a 25-year term policy.

Let me show you one last thing that will really bring my point home. If you take the $125 a month you save in premiums between whole and term and invest it, you will have $165,000. Now that's a savings plan. And the other great thing about it is your loved ones get to keep this money.

Now that I've explained the difference, it is pretty obvious that the term policy is the best policy. I will add a caveat to this, however. If you already have whole life and for some reason (a health issue) you can't get a new term policy, keep what you have. Something is better than nothing.

Now you may be asking "What do I do when the term policy runs out and I'm 50 years old. Won't it cost a lot more to get a new policy?" Yes, it will. But your ultimate goal is to self insure. What do I mean? If you follow the right path to building wealth, by the time the policy runs out, you will have enough money that if something happens to you, your spouse will be okay. Remember, life insurance it there to cover things like mortgages and college if you depart early. If you invest and build wealth for 25 years, you will have plenty to cover this and have a bunch left over. Your house will probably be paid off and your college fund more than likely is fully funded through investments. You will be in a great place financially and life insurance will not be necessary.

My final advice to this young man/lady is to get a new

insurance agent. I always recommend independent agents because they will shop around for you with all available companies and find the best price for you. Based on the question, it sounds like this person has an agent that gets commission for selling whole policies which is usually the case.

Life insurance is a great gift to leave your loved ones and a great legacy to leave. Like all the other things we do in our wealth building journey, we need to make sure we get the most life insurance with the best coverage for the lowest price. Term life is definitely the better choice and a choice I will always recommend. This is one of those great examples where you need to do the math and read the fine print. There is no shame in an agent making money, but there is when he/she is making it at your expense. Find an agent that is looking out for your best interest, not theirs. When you depart this lovely earth, you want to make sure that your loved ones are left with no stress and having a simple life insurance policy, until you are self insured, is a great way to do just that.

Thy Will Be Done

"My husband and I were wondering if we need a will. We have no assets. We do have 2 children, but do we really need to get a will done when we have nothing for them to inherit?"

Everyone over the age of 21 needs a will. Just a super simple will is enough for most – but you do need one. This is an area where most states differ in how they handle things after you depart, but without a will, you are taking a chance on the state getting everything and your loved ones getting nothing. It is imperative that you put your wishes down on paper so that there is no misunderstanding as to what they are.

You may think, like this couple, that you have no assets. But if you have any money or own a car, these are assets and will need to be dealt with. You will also want to make sure that small things like your jewelry, the family Bible, your furniture, that antique grandma gave you, things like that, go where you want them to go. And this isn't just about your children. You may have things that you want your parents to have or your siblings. These items must be put into a will or there is a good chance they will never see them.

And if you have children, it is imperative to lay out the plan of who will take care of them should both parents die. You definitely don't want your kids to end up in foster care for even one minute and without a will, the odds are good that they will.

While we are here on this subject, let me lay out how your debts are handled when you die and how this will affect your wishes. Everything you own must stand for what you owe. This includes anything with your name on it. For example, if your car has your name on it, it would need to be sold to cover your debts if you don't have the cash to do so. If a credit card you use is in your spouse's name only, then you are not responsible, legally, for the debt; therefore, it would not be paid out of your estate.

I am not a lawyer so it is crucial that you speak to one regarding the specifics for your state, again, as they differ from state to state. Everything that I am telling you is in general terms. I highly recommend, also, that you speak to a lawyer to get advice on how to set up things like car titles, house deeds, and bank accounts so that your spouse will have no issues when you depart. The one thing I do know is that what you own has to stand for what you owe and you want to make sure that your spouse or children have no issues in the time of transition after you pass.

Wills are documents that simply lay out your wishes when you depart. There are simple ones and very complicated ones. Most people, even people with a lot of assets, can get by with a simple will. But everyone needs something. This is another inexpensive gift that you can give to your loved one even after you are gone. Don't hesitate to do so.

What Am I Worth?

You are priceless as a human being! You are awesome and can never be replaced. However, in your financial world you do have a worth – what we call a net worth – and you should know what it is. It is a financial snapshot of where you are in this moment.

"My husband and I own our home. It is worth $300,000; however, we do still owe $130,000 on it. We have $127,000 in retirement and $23,500 in debt. Based on all of these numbers, what is our net worth? I hear media talk about millionaires and celebrities and their net worth. Does an average American have a net worth also or is this just for the wealthy?"

Everyone has a net worth even if it is a negative number, which unfortunately many people's are. However, a key to wealth and financial freedom is knowing your net worth at all times. I recalculate ours every 3 months when I do our financial checkup, which we will talk about in a future chapter. It is a very simple formula that gives you a very clear snapshot of your finances and where you need to step it up in order to reach your goals. It can also be a great tool to help you set your financial goals for now and for the future.

First of all, let me clarify one thing about this question that is a common misconception. The lady said that her and her husband "own" their home and then said "we owe" on it.

You do not own something if you still owe on it. If you have a debt against an asset, you do not own it. You have equity in it and the equity is yours, but the item isn't yours until you pay it off. I wanted to clarify this because so many people use this word incorrectly. You will own the house once you have paid it off and the deed is in your hands. Until then, the bank is in control of the amount that you haven't paid off. They own that percentage of the house and they will not relinquish full ownership to you until it is paid in full.

Now, let's look at how to figure out your net worth using our example. All you have to do is use the most basic accounting formula of assets minus liabilities equals net worth. See, I told you it was simple. So let's figure out this couple's net worth together. They have assets totaling $427,000. You do include the value of the home based on what it would sell for because that is the true value of the asset. We are going to include the amount owed on the home in our liabilities number which is $153,500. Therefore, based on the information provided, this couple's net worth is $273,500. This is simply the retirement and the value of the house minus the balance on the house plus the debt they owe otherwise. Simple right? No more excuses for not knowing your net worth.

There are other items to consider that weren't mentioned in this question like cars, cash, stock, etc. You want to include any large assets you have. You don't need to include everything you own like televisions, computers, costume jewelry, etc. But if something can bring value to the equation, you definitely want to include it. This goes the same way for the liability side. You need to include every dollar that you owe to anyone. And you would treat a car with a loan on it the same way you would treat the house. The value of the car (what it would sell for) minus what you owe, even if you are upside down. Again, your net worth is simply the value of everything you have minus the amount owed to everyone.

You want to make sure that you figure out your net worth even if think you have nothing or you owe way more than you have. You always want to have an accurate snapshot of your finances no matter what state they are in. When I started my journey, my net worth was -$197,000. That's not pretty. But it helped me see what I had compared to what I owed and it help me decide to sell some of my assets to lower my debt.

Net worth isn't just for millionaires. It is for everyone. Knowing this number will help you so much on your journey to wealth and financial freedom. It will help you to walk in your truth each and every step of the way and also give you encouragement as you see that number grow in a positive direction.

Hope vs. Planning

I believe that we all need hope. I teach this everyday in every way. But when it comes to our finances, we need to lay out a plan for what we want them to look like and then go about the business of getting it. Hope is wanting something to happen and there is always hope. Anything can happen. "With God all things are possible." But we need to do our part and plan for what we expect. You can't just say "I expect to be a millionaire" and sit back, do nothing, and hope it happens. The hope is the expectation that it can (and it can), but the key is the planning that happens in conjunction with the hope.

"My wife and I are in our late 50's. We haven't always saved the way we should have. We are really hoping that we have enough to live on when we retire. Any suggestions for us at the stage in our lives?"

Did you know that retirement is a government invented concept? In the 19th and early 20th century, people didn't retire. They worked as long as they were able. But in the early 20th century, when the social security system part of our government came along, people all the sudden jumped on this bandwagon of retirement – basically, at a certain age you stop working. To me, that is the same as saying, at a certain age, everyone dies. That is silly right. Well, basically society says this. At age 65, you should retire. But why?

I am a firm believer in working in your passion and enjoying life. With this concept, there is never a reason to retire. Sure, maybe you slow down as you need to based on your personal needs, but to stop working and do nothing seems a little life draining. If more people worked in their passion, they would want to work no matter how old they are. Warren Buffett is 87. And he could have retired when he was 40. But what would he have done for the rest of his life. Betty White is 96 and still acting. Sure, she acts much less than she did, but she still does it because it is what she loves.

You need to plan to have the exact life you want. Maybe you won't get everything, but you should look at what you really want, what makes you truly happy and go after it. I am 48 years old and I love what I do. I will probably die on stage at the age of 90 telling a group of people how to get out of debt and build wealth. I'm not sitting here looking forward to 65 so I can stop working. My husband and I love to travel. He is 61. We aren't sitting here saying "Well, in 4 years we can start traveling." We travel now. What the heck does 65 have to do with anything?

What it is is a magic number that everyone uses to plan to stop working. But if you enjoy what you do, why would you stop. Of course, life can change things. Maybe you end up with some health issues that may slow you down or change your path, but we should never give up doing what we can do and what we love to do. I know people who travel in wheelchairs and have a blast. I also know people who love to travel but give it up because they think they can't travel anymore. Your attitude about life is everything.

My answer to the couple who asked this question was more about where they see themselves in the next 20 years and less about their retirement funds. Saving and investing are something that you should do always. Investing is a great way for your money to make money without any effort from you. Compound interest is your best friend in the savings realm. But I really wanted to know what their plans were? Were they planning to retire or retiring at age 65 and hoping they could live? Life is about planning as much as you can and having hope that it will work. If plan A doesn't work, don't panic. There are 25 more letters in the alphabet.

There is always hope. I can never say that enough. There is great hope for the couple asking our question. But part of that hope is in the planning. We can't just hope we become wealthy; we must plan to become wealthy, but when our plan goes off course, there is always hope that it will work out. Plan for your retirement and when it seems impossible, keep hoping because there are always unseen answers when we do. But don't plan to retire and give up. Keep on living. Keep on doing something. Volunteer, change careers, love on grandchildren, anything that brings you joy. And if you love what you do, keep doing it. 65 is not a magic number. It is simply a government based guideline that it is okay to ignore. Live your life everyday to the fullest and never show up to the funeral before it's time.

Social Security

"My wife and are in our early 60's and we aren't sure exactly how Social Security works and when the best time to file for it would be?"

Social security is a government program that has been around since the early 1900's. It is a program that you pay into every year that you work and when you reach a certain age, you can begin receiving payments back from the government. Basically it is an investment plan that you have no control over. I'm not saying that to be negative against the program – I am saying that to remind you that it is government run and they control everything about it – how much you pay in, how much you receive and when. I always recommend people to have their own investments for their future because at any time this program could change or even go away. If you have your own investments, then any money you collect from social security becomes gravy. It is never a good idea to rely on anyone for your future and especially not the government.

As of the writing of this book, the three ages to choose from to start drawing Social Security are 62, 67 and 70. Of course, you want to look into your specifics based on your year of birth, but here is the general synopsis. 67 years old is the sweet spot – official retirement age with full benefit. If you choose to start drawing at 62, you are going to loose a decent percentage of that money. However, if you wait until 70, that benefit will go up. Anytime after 70, the benefit is the same. In general, I always recommend to hold out as long as you can to get the maximum benefit which is age 70. I would only start drawing before that if I absolutely had to to live, which I know is the case for some people. Just like with any investments, you want to hold on as long as you can to get the most out of them. Even if you retire (stop working) at age 62 or even younger, you don't have to file if you have the money to live on in the meantime. This is one reason you want to make sure you invest early for your future.

You can always go to the social security website - https://www.ssa.gov/myaccount/ - and look at your specific draw amounts for each of the three ages. I do this every year as a part of our financial checkups. I print out both mine and my husband's and add it to our legacy book so that at anytime we know what the most recent amount is.

If you have a job that issues you a W-2 at the end of the year, your contributions are automatically taken out and made. If you own your own business or receive a 1099 for work you have done, your contribution will be based on your profit and this amount is part of your tax on your tax return. If you are a homemaker or do not work for other reasons, you will not show contributions for those years. Keep this in mind when laying out your retirement numbers. Again, I highly recommend looking at social security as a bonus and making sure, through your investments, that you have enough to live on when and if you are no longer receiving a paycheck.

And just a side note – I would say the same thing about pensions. Most companies no longer have pensions for current employees. Some state and federal governments still have some sort of pension in place and there are companies who are still paying employees who retired with them years ago. If you are receiving a pension, I highly recommend that you look at that as gravy too. You never want to put control of your finances in the hands of someone else. What if a large portion of your income was a pension and all of the sudden that pension went away. You may be saying "Well that would never happen to me", but I would encourage you to talk to anyone from Bethlehem Steel. It can happen to you. This is why the money you need to live on should come from your investments and anything extra from any other source is just a sweet bonus. This way, if it does go away, you are still okay with no worries. You don't want to be 75 and have to go get a job simply because your pension was taken away. Prepare for that and in turn, you will be sitting pretty with the pension and the social security as extra money.

There is a place for social security but it can't be the answer to your financial future. Plan, save and invest for your own financial needs and enjoy the gravy as it flows in.

Saving Grace

"We are just starting to get out of debt and we were wondering where and how much to save as we move forward including regular savings, emergency funds and retirement."

Savings accounts and money markets nowadays do not have anywhere near the rate of return that they used to. However, even making one percent is better than keeping it under your mattress. On a $20,000 emergency fund, that is an extra $200 a year. And free money is free money. The key when it comes to your emergency fund savings is you need quick access to it; therefore, you will need to keep it in some type of savings or money market account – at a local bank, credit union, or even a reputable online bank like Ally or Capital One. As of the writing of this book, both of the online options are paying an average of 1%. Sometimes, if your balance is over $10,000, you can yield a little more. You just need to research it.

What I have always done that works for me and I always recommend it to my clients is I keep my starter emergency fund ($1,000) in a savings account at the same bank as my checking account, even if it doesn't pay interest. This is to ensure that I have access to it in the event of a super emergency where I need cash immediately. I then keep my 6 month (a year in my case) emergency fund in another bank where it can make money and where I have access to it quickly when needed. I personally use Capital One, but there are many to choose from. You just want to make sure the transfer process is 1-2 business days so there is no delay in getting the money you need for your emergency. It is so easy with online banking now to transfer money back and forth quickly. We have already covered emergency funds and how much to save and when, but just to recap – you want to save $1,000 first, get out of debt, and then save at minimum 3-6 months, definitely leaning toward the six and eventually you want to try to reach one year. Having a year's worth of expenses sitting in a bank account in case you need it will bring you a peace like nothing else can.

Now, as for investing, I am not a financial advisor and I will not even start to give investing advice. However, I will tell you a little of what I learned to guide you in the direction that you need to go. First of all, you must find a financial advisor that is more concerned about you as a client than they are about their commissions. One way they show this is by listening to you and teaching you about the products and funds available and then letting you make the decision that is best for you. If they are over pushing a product, odds are they are getting a commission on it and it probably won't work for you. Do your research, ask questions and don't be afraid to shop around and get multiple opinions. You don't want too many because that can get very confusing, but two definitely wouldn't hurt. A colleague of mine, Dave Ramsey, has a tool on his website to help with this process. The people recommended there have been vetted by him and his team and they encompass the teaching and not the selling. Check out his website for more information..

As for the amount you put in, the industry standard recommendation is 15% and I do agree this is a great place to start. However, the more you invest, the more money your money can make. So I would set a goal of 15% as a minimum, but always be open to investing more in order to receive more free money. Also, make sure that you are taking advantage of a company 401K if they have a match. The company match, say it's 2%, is again free money. You never want to leave free money on the table.

There are also other products such as real estate that you can invest in as well, as long as you have the cash to do so. You can always put your money in a mutual fund until it reaches the amount you need to pay cash for a property. Cash will bring you a bargain, keep you from having debt on a property and help you to have more equity right out of the gate on the property.

Savings in any form is important. If you spend every dollar you have, you will eventually not have money when an emergency occurs or when you want to do something big in the future. Having that emergency fund savings first is the most important thing. This way you will never have to use debt to cover life when it happens. But once that is taken care of, you have an awesome opportunity to use your money to make even more money. This is a great step towards making sure you can do all the wonderful things that you want to do in your future years.

2 Birds – 1 Stone

"We are in the process of paying off our debt. We are 35 years old and we have about $20,000 left on our debt. We expect to be debt free in 2 years or less. Should we stop our 401K contributions to ramp that up or keep contributing during this time?"

Some of my colleagues feel very strong one way or the other on this subject and neither point of view is wrong. There are pros and cons to stopping all investing and savings and focusing on the debt and there are pros and cons to continuing these contributions while getting out of debt. This is one of the cases where I believe the difference isn't very much; therefore, this should be a personal choice. But I do want to take a few minutes and look at the pros and cons so you can make the best decision possible for your goals.

You absolutely can do both. The couple in our question is on course to be out of debt in 2 years; therefore, for them, I don't believe that stopping their contributions is necessary. However, if they really want to be out of debt in a year, then yes, stopping their contributions for that year is no big deal. The big question for me is always how long until you are going to be out of debt. If it is going to take you 5 years, I wouldn't want you to stop contributing for that amount of time. That is a long span of time to put your investing on hold. And if you have a matching 401K, I would contribute at least up to the match because you never want to leave free money on the table. Most companies match around 2% so investing this 2% while getting out of debt won't change much, but it will gain you the free 2% over the course of that time.

Another factor that makes this a personal choice is focus. Many people believe that focusing on one thing at a time helps you succeed faster in all areas. Therefore, if you focus simply on paying off debt, putting every dollar you have toward it, you can get out of debt quickly and then start investing more since you have no debt. This is the way for many people; it was for me. And if you are like this, then you absolutely want to stop all investing and focus on getting out of debt. Once you are out of debt, you will be in a great place financially. This will mean that you can start investing more to make up for the short time that you missed. However, if you are the type of person who can focus on two things as once, by all means, go for it.

You also want to consider your age when making this choice. Our couple is 35 years old. This means that they would stop contributing a small amount for 2 years and then invest more for 30 years. For them, stopping isn't an issue because they have time to make it up. However, if you are in your fifties when you decide to get out of debt, you probably don't want to stop contributing since you have less time to make it up.

See what I mean about personal. There are hundreds of scenarios and in each one, you have to look at all of the factors to make the best decision for you. I never teach one way and say that is the only way. I've seen too many people fail in those scenarios and it is simply because that was something that didn't work for them. The goals and concepts of personal finance are all consistent – getting out of debt, saving for the future, never overpaying for what you are getting, etc. – but the strategy to accomplish these goals is always different. And my mission has always been to show you all of your options so that you can find the one that works for you. So many times people make bad decisions simply because they don't have enough information and they don't take into consideration what is going to work for them. Something that works for someone else may not work for you and that is okay. God made us all different; therefore, we must always do what is best for us and what will move us forward in our lives.

Investing is never a bad thing. This is always the best way for your money to make more money. As I said before, compound interest is your best friend in the savings realm. However, it never hurts to press the pause button on investing for a short time in order to reach such an important goal as getting out of debt. I definitely wouldn't pause it for any other reason because you are leaving too much money behind when you do. And I definitely would only do it for a short time – 1-2 years tops. If you are not careful, you will try to convince yourself that you can catch up later and you will look up and realize later never came. Which brings me to my last point, if you do decide to pause, make a very specific plan on the amount of money and the amount of time and stick to it. You don't want to pause it for one day more than you need to get out of debt.

You can kill two birds with one stone. You can get out of debt and still invest. The choice is yours. If you decide to pause, lay out the plan and stick to it. And if you decide to do both, look everywhere else in your budget to find the money to get out of debt as quickly as possible. Once you are out of debt, the investing possibilities are endless – to infinity and beyond.

Good or Bad Thing?

So many times in our lives we look at something as a bad thing and then we look back later and see that it was a good thing. Our question is a prime example of this exact thing.

"I lost my job of 20 years a couple of months ago. I have been looking for a job in a similar field and I just haven't had any luck. I'm not sure what I am doing wrong. Is it because I am older – I'm in my late 40's and there are younger people applying for the same jobs. Any advice would be great."

Losing your job can be a real blow to your self esteem even if you hated your job. First of all, most of us need our jobs, so there is the panic that sets in when we lose ours. And most of us feel like we are good at our jobs so we can't figure out why they got rid of us. Even in layoff situations, we can take a big hit emotionally. But after we have about a 10-minute pity party, we need to start looking at this as an opportunity rather than a bad thing. If you were not working in your passion, now is the time to do just that. And if you were, maybe it is time to move forward and try a different approach. Either way, this is a great opportunity for you if you can envision it.

First, let me address the issue of you not getting the jobs you are applying for. It is a whole different world now than it used to be. The last time I went looking for a job, I got a newspaper everyday and sent résumés to any and every job that I could. Financially, I couldn't afford to be without a job. I also signed up with temp agencies and took every job I could including delivering newspapers just to make money. But do you notice one thing here – the desperation I felt. If you do not have an emergency fund in place, losing your job can make you very desperate and this can show when you are interviewing. If you have an emergency fund in place, you know that you have a little bit of time; therefore, you aren't desperate and you interview very differently. If this is the case and you are desperate because you don't have an emergency fund, find something simple to do for a short time to bring in money so that you can relax enough to interview well and come across as confident. Also, this allows you to not take a job out of desperation and start the vicious cycle of job hating all over again.

This is also a huge opportunity that many people miss. It is a great opportunity to start your own business. This isn't the case for everyone and not everyone is designed to run a business, but if it is something that you have considered and you think it might be something you love, this is a great opportunity to do it. You will need to start it without debt, so you still may need odd jobs to fund the business and pay your bills, but at least you will be on your way to living your dream.

There are also businesses that you can start just to make extra money like dog walking, cutting lawns, babysitting, and house cleaning. These businesses simply require a business card and some hard work and word of mouth to get the word out. These may not be dream jobs, but they are things that you can start in order to make money until you land the dream job.

Age can be a good thing and a bad thing. With age comes wisdom and experience. Therefore, you bring more to the table than a younger person would. However, the older you are, the less time you will have with the company. If this is a concern, they might look for someone a little younger for the position. Either way, you have one job. Convince them that you are the right person for the job. Speak confidently about what you bring to the table, what you can do for them, and why you are the only choice. Notice I said confident, not cocky. Just know what your assets are and sell them.

I have had more than my fair share of job losses over my working lifetime, so I know exactly what you are going through. I wish I knew then what I know now and what I am telling you. Of course, then I wouldn't be here serving you on a daily basis which is my dream job. Always know what your passion is, what your dream job looks like, and go after it. And if you find yourself in a job loss situation, look at it as an opportunity not a misfortune. Take the lemons of life and make award winning lemonade.

Change is Good

"We have had a lot of things changing in our lives recently and I am not sure what to do. My husband wants to start his own business. My daughter is leaving for college. I am no longer happy at my job. We seem to be spending more and accumulating debt in the process. How do I deal with so much change at one time? I don't know where to begin. I would like to just stick my head in the sand."

Change is a good thing; however, it can be extremely uncomfortable for most. We get so used to our little world that we live in that when something changes it is hard for us to see how it can be better. I recently went through my daughter going away to college as well. It was different, not having her in the same house day after day, but I decided to focus on the positive parts of this transition – more date nights, more travel with my husband, only 2 people to cook for – and not the negative. And with technology today, you can see them anytime you want. I probably talk to my daughter more now than I ever did before. She texts me at least once a day and calls about 5 times a week. We have always been close, but the change has only made us closer.

When change is occurring, even something that in the natural is bad, like an illness or a job loss, we must always look at the positive in the situation. Sometimes it can be hard to find, but it is in there. When you look at a change as an opportunity instead of a problem, your outlook is completely different.

Some changes can't be controlled and some can. For example, in our question, starting a business, happiness in the job, and accumulating debt are all things that can be controlled. Many times, when change happens is when we tend to lose control, but it is vital that we keep control at all times. There is no reason why the three things she mentioned can't be done, but they need to be done in a way that is best for them. The daughter going off to college cannot be controlled and is a situation that they will have to decide to make the most of. And by the way, it is completely your decision to make the most of it – that is in your control. I am going to go one step further – I am willing to bet that the daughter leaving for college is what brought about the other three changes. As they transitioned into this new season, they weren't as prepared as they should have been for the emotional and financial changes; therefore, all of the sudden they want to do something different or spend money to fix it.

This isn't the answer and neither is sticking your head in the sand. I know to many this is going to sound silly or too hard, but a positive mindset can change your whole world when the seasons of life change. We are all going to be faced with change. We are all going to be faced with things we didn't expect to happen. We are all going to be faced with tragedy and loss. But how we handle these situations is the key to succeeding in life.

5 years ago, my godmother fell down the concrete stairs outside her church. Ever since that day, she has had dementia. On that day, we lost the mother that we had known our whole lives, but we were still blessed to have her with us physically. We all had to learn a new way. All six of us handled it in a different way. But we are a pretty positive

group so we have made it through. One day, just a few weeks after this happened, my sister and I were visiting mom in rehab. All of the sudden she asked us if we were packed. My sister asked where were we going and she said Hawaii. We were like "Yes!". A little later she asked us again if we were packed because we had to get to the train station. In her mind, we were taking a train to Hawaii. We could have been sad about the fact that our mom was thinking that. Be we decided to be happy at the silliness of the idea. We laughed so hard, we even got mom laughing.

Please don't misunderstand – it is still very hard for us to watch our mom struggle the way she does for thoughts and words. But I personally try to focus on the positive things in our situation. You see, her accident was out of anyone's control. The only choice I had was how was I going to deal with this major change in my life.

This is how life is – one minute everything can be great and the next, you can get kicked in the teeth. But how you react to the change is completely up to you. My advice for the lady who sent me the question – deal first with the transition of your daughter going to school. Find all of the positive things and when something negative pops up, replace it with positive. Make an effort to be a part of her life and never let her feel like she has disappointed you by going away to college. This is her life and she has made the best choice for her right now. Support her in that every way you can.

Once you are good in that area, take a good hard look at the other areas. I would start with the money because if you don't get the debt under control, you are just going to keep digging a bigger hole. And you don't need to change careers until you get a plan for clearing up this debt. Then you and your husband need to take a good, hard look at your jobs and see why you want to change them and why you aren't happy. It may be something you can change. And remember, change is good. But if at the end of it all, you find out you aren't working in your passion and you want to pursue it, by all means do so. Develop a plan and go for it. So many times the real problem disguises itself in another area. Jobs, money and relationships are always the main targets. When you are feeling out of sorts in one area, do a little soul research to get to the root of the real problem. Then work your way out from there.

Change is most always a good thing. But whether we see it or not – that is something else. I challenge you to find the good in every change where you can. And if you can't, accept the change as a good thing and move forward accordingly. You are the only one who can control how change is going to affect you. You are the author of your own story. Write a best seller!

God's View of Money

"My husband and I are people of faith. However, I noticed that there isn't a lot of talk about God and money in our church. How does God feel about money? What is His view on things like buying a car, debt, etc. ?"

God actually feels very strong about this subject. The subject of money is referenced over 2000 times in the Bible. That seems important to me. My favorite verse I love to use when talking about how God feels about money is Deuteronomy 8:18 – where He says that we have all been given the ability to have and obtain wealth.

God loves us and like any parent, He wants only the best for us. God understands that money is needed in order to do things, help others, and fulfill many of the desires of our heart. However, many times, He cautions us about our heart when it comes to money. He wants to make sure that our hearts are pure and giving and not greedy.

We have all been given the ability to obtain wealth – this is visible in the simple formula of investing $100 a month from age 25-65 will yield you $1.7 million. We all have $100 – yes, all. However, many of us spend everything we have on other things and don't invest the $100 which is why everyone is not wealthy. If you choose to spend your $100 on something else instead of saving and investing it, you are choosing to not have wealth. Money is not evil – the love of money is. The more money we have, the more we can give, help those in need and provide for our needs and our desires easily. This is why God has given us each the ability. However, like any gift, if it isn't used, it doesn't produce any good. You must use the wisdom God has given you in order to actually obtain wealth. It's not a secret formula; there is no money tree. Wealth is obtained by making wise, godly decisions. Building wealth requires action.

Now, what about debt – how does God feel about debt. He is very clear about this as well. Proverbs 22:7 clearly states that the borrower is a slave to the lender. He also states to never owe anyone anything but love. There are more verses, but these two alone say enough for you to understand God doesn't agree with debt. God doesn't like it when we are stressed. Having debt can make you very stressed at times - taking away your peace, the peace that He sent His Son to give.

God isn't specific about purchases in the Bible. For example, you won't see a verse about which car to buy. Through a lot of prayer and study, I truly believe this is because God doesn't care what we do with our money. Everyone is different and has different desires. Some people love to travel, some people like big houses, some people like nice cars – we all like different things. It isn't about the things. It is about how we get them. If the only way to buy a car is to go into debt, then you shouldn't buy the car. If the only way to buy a house is to do a 100% loan, then you shouldn't buy the house.

God has instructed us to live on less than we make, to give and to save. If we do as He has instructed, we can have anything that we can afford. I always say you can have anything, just not everything.

When it comes to money, God is way more concerned about your heart than your bank account. Everything we have is His anyway. We are just stewards – money managers – of what He wants us to have. As it says in one of Jesus's parables, we are going to be given based on how we handle what we already have. If we handle what we have well, then we will be given more. If not, we won't. I noticed this principle when I started making better financial decisions. As I started paying off debt, I would receive financial blessings here and there to help me. But when I wasn't making good decisions, I noticed I lost my peace and my blessings.

Make it your goal to handle your money as if God is watching everything – because He is. Just like you would any job you have, manage God's money well and you will be promoted in that area more and more. God wants the best for you and wants very much to give you the desires of your heart. Prove to Him you can handle it and watch the blessings flow.

Garbage In, Garbage Out

"I saw in your first book that the first chapter was about attitude. I didn't realize that attitude had anything to do with money. Could you explain the connection please?"

I am always happy to explain this connection because it is one that a lot of people don't make very easily – and many still struggle even after they hear it. Attitude is defined as a way of thinking that is reflected in one's actions. This means that how you think shows up in your actions. For example, many people never believe that they will be wealthy and most of those people never will be. This isn't because of social inequality, has nothing to do with what side of the tracks they were born on, and isn't dependent on their income. It is about their attitude.

They may not see this clearly because we are trained as a society to blame certain things for the fact that we aren't where we would love to be financially – the government, our boss, the bank, anyone but ourselves. But the truth is we are where we are because of the decisions we have made and the attitude we have regarding them.

I heard a story today that may help a little and I hope will not only reflect what I am talking about, but will also give you hope in this area. When Katrina hit, there was a maid who worked for a huge hotel chain. The management asked the staff to stay and told them that if they took care of the guests, the hotel would take care of them. As the storm got closer, the maid had her family come to the hotel where she was. The staff helped each and every guest to make sure they were safe. Eventually, everyone – guests and staff alike – were bused to Baton Rouge to a hotel owned by the same chain. Again, the staff were told, if you help us take care of our guests, we will take care of you. When everything was said and done, the management gave each staff member a list of cities where they had hotels and offered to move them there and give them a full-time job as their hotel wasn't going to be open for quite some time. The lady picked Texas where she moved, started her new job, found a church, made friends and was even given a car to start her new life.

The amazing thing about this story is that not once did she complain. She did what she was asked trusting that everything would be okay. And it turned out better than she could have ever imagined. She had actually been hoping to move to Texas one day, but wasn't sure how to make that happen. This beautiful lady never lost her smile, never lost her hope and never had a negative attitude. She remained positive and positive results followed.

Most likely someone else was going through the exact same thing at the same time, but received different results because they chose to have a negative attitude instead of a positive one. Yes, I said chose. Your attitude is a choice. It is not something you are born with. It is something that is developed. The good news with that means that if you happen to lean a little more toward the negative side currently, you can change things and move the needle in a positive direction.

What we put in our minds and choose to think about is what will mold our attitude – garbage in, garbage out. Like I said before, if you believe you will never win in the area of your finances, odds are you never will. Not because you can't –

simply because your attitude is going to direct your decisions.

When I was sitting on my living room floor 19 years ago, I had a very negative attitude. I was a nice person, but my attitude sucked. I thought it was everybody else's fault I was where I was. And when something happened, I automatically got defensive, mad and negative about it. I had to do a major overhaul once I realized this principle, but it saved my life. I can promise you I would not be where I am today if I was still holding on to my negative attitude. I would not be debt free, a successful business owner, author and speaker, a wonderful mother and an awesome wife. Honestly, I would probably still be where I was 19 years ago. I may have moved the needle a little, but nothing like what I ended up doing once I took a good hard look at myself and grasped this attitude concept.

As my friend Zig Ziglar used to say, "Your attitude determines your altitude." It's that simple – you will go as far in life as your attitude takes you. As we have talked about numerous times already, personal finance is 10% math and 90% emotions. This is one area that falls under the emotion category and will have a direct effect on your money.

It's pretty simple – if you want your finances to change, change your attitude in a positive way. Doing this will take you further than anything else you can possibly do.

Government Savings Plan

"My husband and I are getting a large tax refund this year and we were wondering what would be the best thing to do with it. It is about $3,000. We do have about $14,000 in debt and $40,000 in retirement. "

First, let me clarify something. Tax refunds are your money – money that you have overpaid to the government over the last 12 months. Refunds are not a gift or bonus from the government. If you receive a refund every year, you are basically giving the government your money to hold for a year at 0% interest – this is a horrible savings plan by the way.

Your goal when it comes to taxes is to get as close to break-even as you possibly can – you don't owe them and they don't owe you. The best way to do this is to go to the IRS website and use their withholding calculator to determine what your deduction status should be. Most people, when they fill out their W-4 with an employer, put the same deductions as their tax return and most of the time, this ends up taking out more than you need. This is why so many people end up with tax refunds year after year.

But wouldn't you love to keep your money and pay the government only what you owe? In our sample question, this couple is paying $250 extra every month in taxes. What could you do with $250 extra every month? For many of you, this would rock your world. And if you happen to be out of debt and want to invest this money, you would be able to turn $250 a month into $325,000 over the course of 25 years. Much better than $0 with the government savings plan, right?

I know that it can be an awesome feeling every year when you get that check. For many of you, it's like winning the lottery. However, now that you know it is your money, it's not like winning the lottery. It is like someone taking your money for one year and then, once a year, giving it back to you, again with no interest. This is not a good financial plan.

So how do you solve this problem without owing a big tax bill? First, you use the withholding calculator that I mentioned to get your actual deduction status. Then, fill out a new W-4 with your employer. I would recommend doing this every year, around February, to make sure you are still on track. And right now, as I am writing this, major tax laws are changing, so I would do a checkup every 3 months just to make sure you are still on track. You definitely don't want any surprises. You can use the withholding calculator anytime and change your W-4 as many times as you need. Again, your ultimate goal is to owe the IRS nothing and for them to owe you nothing.

Now, if you still want to overpay and get that huge check every year, make sure you don't treat it like a windfall. It is money you have overpaid and money that is part of your income. So, you will want to treat it as such. When you get it, put it toward the next financial goal that you have. In the example question, I would recommend they apply the whole check toward debt if they have an emergency fund started. Becoming debt free should be their next financial goal based on the information I was given.

My job is always to give you the facts. When it comes to tax refunds, I have found that so many people don't realize it is their money. They file what the W-4 suggests and in doing so they receive a check every year from the government. Most people don't know that they can decide what is deducted from their check. Every person who works will owe a set amount of tax. I always recommend simply paying them what you owe and divide it over all of your paychecks. However, the government loves for you to pay more so that they can use your money during the year without paying interest. Whatever you decide is okay as long as you no longer have the delusion of who's money it is.

There is one exception to this that I want to make sure I mention. Sometimes there are special circumstances where you will receive a tax credit on your tax return. This is money from the government and is an incentive to do something or financial help in offsetting a large expense. For example, as of last year, there is a tax deduction for adopting a baby. This is a credit and is extra money the government is giving you to offset the cost of adoption. In these situations, you don't want to change anything because they are one time credits. Keep this in mind when using the withholding calculator. One time credits are not to be included in your withholding status.

Two final thoughts: Make sure that you do a checkup with the withholding calculator throughout the year to make sure you are on track and if you do get a refund, use it on the next step in your financial plan – not as free money. It is your money. Treat it with respect.

FICO 101

"We know what our credit scores are; however, we have no clue what they mean or how they are figured out. We need to improve our score which is currently 650 and 667. Would you please explain what FICO is and how the score is figured out?"

FICO used to be used occasionally to figure out whether you were credit worthy or not. Today it is used for everything – from getting a loan to getting a job. It is your financial reputation. It shows lenders everything about you so that they can make a judgement of whether to loan you money or not. The problem is it is all computer generated. They have completely taken the human factor out of lending. What I mean by that is years ago, if you were behind due to job loss or a medical situation, that was taken into consideration. Today it is not. If you are a college football fan, consider it the reverse of the BCS ranking system. Everything used to be done by computer. But in the last 3 years, they have used a committee to determine who goes to the championship games. The committee considers everything from strength of schedule to injuries to stats from the game. It isn't black and white – win or lose. And that is the way credit used to be. But now, it is black and white. In the financial world, you are just a number.

So, how is that number calculated. 35% is your payment history, 30% is the amount you owe versus the amount of credit you have access to, 15% is length of credit history,

10% is new accounts and 10% is types of credit. As we talked about before, if you already have a credit score, the best thing you can do is to make decisions that will move you forward and will improve your score. It is challenging, but not impossible, to get a zero credit score once one has been established. It will take a lot of time because you have to wait for every category to reach zero. Let's look at each category to see what you can do raise that area up and in the process, raise your finances as well.

- **Payment history** – This is simply paying your bills on time. This has nothing to do with how much you pay. As long as you pay the minimum required on time, this will always be 100%. If this has been a problem for you in the past, start now paying everything on time. As you saw, this has the biggest impact. And if you have a medical bill or another bill without a minimum, if you can't pay in full, work with the business to pay what they want to keep your account current. When lenders or anyone sees late payment, they see someone who can't handle their finances and someone who isn't organized.

- **Credit utilization** – This is the amount you owe versus the amount of credit you have access to – your limit. If this is below 30%, your credit is considered good and if it is below 10%, your credit is considered great. Remember, we have already talked about this regarding debt. Just because you pay your bill in full every month doesn't mean your credit will be good in this area. The amount reported is your statement amount. Keep that in mind when trying to improve your number. There are two ways to improve this number – pay down what you owe or raise your limit and don't use it. Either way or both will improve your score.

- **Length of credit history** – This is an average of the oldest debt and the newest debt. You have no control in this number except to stop going into debt. If you got a credit card 5 years ago, your score would be good. But if you got a new card now, your average would go to 2.5 years which is not good. Keep this in mind when applying for anything new.

- **New accounts** – This is the number of new accounts you have within the last two years. This is also where inquires come into play because the computer assumes that every inquiry turns into debt. Again, the best way to keep this number low is to stop applying. No inquires, no new accounts, great credit score.

- **Types of credit** – There is more than just credit cards when it comes to credit. This part of your score likes to see a nice mixture – credit cards, personal loans, student loans, auto loans, etc. Interestingly, as long as you have credit cards you are good with this category. However, if all you have is student loans, you will show negatively in this calculation.

Now, where do you go to find out your score and see what you need to work on. The best website is Credit Karma and it is absolutely free. It gives you an updated score for TransUnion and Equifax once a week and shows you the breakdown of your score so that you can see where you need to improve. There is another free one – Credit Sesame – which does the same for Equifax only. I would never pay for a credit score. Many credit cards and banks are offering this as a free service now as well.

However, you gain your free access, take a good look at your score and your numbers. And then look at the breakdown to see where you need to improve and use the tips I have shared as a place to start. Once I started paying attention to my score and what it meant, I raised my score 100 points in one year. It is all about knowledge and not just accepting what others tell you. Your financial decisions control your FICO score. Make better decisions, raise your score. It is that simple.

Report Card

We talked about how your FICO score is used and how it is calculated. Now, let's talk about the report itself, as what is on it is vital to your score.

"How do I find out what is on my credit report? My score is lower than I think it should be and I would like to look at the details so I can see if something is wrong."

Just like your FICO score, you never want to pay for a credit report. You have the right to see your credit report once a year from each of the three reporting bureaus – Equifax, TransUnion, and Experian. If you go to www.annualcreditreport.com, you can receive a free detailed report once a year. You will need to answer a few security questions so that they know it is you and then you will be able to view and print your report. If you have never looked at your report before, I would get all three at one time; however, going forward, I would spread them out over the year. I do one every four months. Whether you get them all at once or spread out, just make sure you get them and make sure you are using the free website above. Many websites say they are free, but will end up charging you later. Never give them your credit card when you sign up. This is a sure sign they are not free.

Now that you have your report, what do you do with it? The first thing is to take the time to look at everything, and I mean everything, for accuracy. You want to even include names, dates, addresses and places of employment. These are harder to change, but you want to make sure your report is as accurate as possible.

If you find an error, you want to correct it as soon as possible as it may be affecting your score. Some things are easy to dispute and some things are much harder and may require lots of time working with the reporting agency. So you want to prioritize what is affecting your score and what is window dressing and can be addressed later.

First, you want to focus on the accounts and their status. Look at the account to make sure it is yours and make sure they are reporting the correct information regarding payment status and balance. Keep in mind they may be a month behind depending on when they were reported. So if you paid off a debt this month, it may take several months for it to show zero. Also, keep in mind that accounts stay on your report for a time even if you close them. Let's say you pay off your auto loan, it will continue to show for years after you pay it off so don't expect it to go away. As long as the account is in good standing, it will help your score so it's okay for it to stay. If you are showing collection accounts on your report, make sure you look to see who the original lender was. You also have the right to request a statement from the collector. The addresses are on the report. You can only dispute things that you truly do not owe – not things you think you shouldn't owe.

After you have gone over the report with a fine tooth comb, you will want to dispute anything that isn't yours. If something is being reported incorrectly number wise, you will need to address that with the lender. Disputing is only for items that need to be removed because they do not belong to you. This can happen very easily which is why you want to check it every year. A few years ago there was a gentleman in our area who had the exact name as my husband. My husband ended up with a lien against him because they were reporting it everywhere even though the social security number didn't match. We had it removed from the report and from the lender once we proved the different socials. Many times lenders are grasping at straws and you need to protect yourself from unwarranted reporting.

Each reporting agency has a different procedure for disputing an item. It is easy to find on their respective websites. You need to just visit their website and begin a dispute for every incorrect item. Some of them will let you dispute everything at one time, others want one at a time. Just follow the instructions and you will be fine. Once you file the dispute, they have thirty days to get back to you with a result. It is usually sooner but some items do take the entire time. This is because in most cases, they reach out to the other party to prove the validity. If they can't prove it is your debt and a valid debt, it will be removed. If they can, odds are it won't because you do owe the money. This is not a procedure to remove something just because you don't like what it says. This is only for removing legitimate mistakes on your report.

If they don't remove it and you truly don't owe it, you will want to make your case to them in writing with proof of why this isn't your debt. Again, you want your report to be accurate so even though it can be tedious, you want to do what you need to do to get the item removed. As a ray of hope for you, in all my years of helping clients with this and doing my own, I have never had to fight for it. If you truly don't owe it, they will remove it.

We talked about how your FICO score reflects your financial reputation. Your credit report is your report card. It is a detailed account of every decision you have made financially. And just like you would any report card, you want to make sure that everything is being recorded accurately so that you can get the best possible grade available. And just like a report card, in the areas where you are struggling and not getting the best grades, you should work really hard to do everything you can to bring that grade up. Straight A's is always the goal. Do your best to achieve it!

Financial Checkups

Just like we go to the doctor and dentist for checkups, we need to perform checkups on our finances periodically in order to keep them healthy. Never put your finances on auto pilot. In order to win in the area of your money, it is important that you pay attention and always get the most value for what you need.

"How often should I change and update my policies when it comes to auto insurance? I've had the same company for 20 years and I'm wondering should I be looking around for something better."

Definitely – always be looking for the best price. Unfortunately, companies are moving away from loyalty discounts in many areas. So, don't assume you are getting the best rate simply because you have been with a company for a length of time. This goes with any of your expenses. Cable companies are the worst when it comes to this. They reserve all the deals for new customers and won't give a lot of discounts for loyal customers. But you don't have to accept this. You can change companies, as long as you aren't under a contract, or cut the cable bill completely. Always shop around for every expense you have. Never pay more than you should simply because you didn't want to take the time to shop. And with the internet, it's not very hard to get the numbers you need to make the best decisions.

Once you have your numbers, I would try to get your

current company to match it. Let them know you are shopping around and you wanted to see if they would match the price before you leave. If they don't, and many won't so don't be upset, simply go with another company. For most standard items, the coverage and customer service are about the same. Therefore, the only factor is price. Only pay more if you are truly getting your money's worth with the difference. A great example of this is car insurance. You will get a lower rate at some of the lower companies, but your coverage and service will not be the same. Don't sacrifice that to get a low price. However, when you put the top companies together – they all have great customer service and coverage – then price is usually the deciding factor. For example, if you were comparing between State Farm and Geico and Geico was less expensive for the same coverage, you should go with Geico. You won't get better for the difference you will pay.

The author of our question asked how often should they shop around for car insurance. I include this in my financial checkup process. There are several things that need to be looked at throughout the year to make sure they are still in a healthy state. Let's look at them now.

- **Insurance** – Auto insurance should be shopped every 6 months, about one month before your current policy expires. You can do this on the internet, but I highly recommend using an independent insurance agent because they can shop all of the companies available, some who only make their insurance available through them. I would take a look at your health, life and long-term care insurance at least once a year, also using an independent agent.

- **Expenses** – All expenses should be looked at monthly, but I suggest taking a close look every three months to see if there is anything you can do to lower the bill. Sometimes you may be in a contract, like with cable or cell phones, but there are always ways to cut back even before the end of the contract.

- **Net Worth** – You want to determine this every month. This will help you to keep a clear picture of your assets and your liabilities and will help you see how your investments are doing as well.

- **Investments** – You don't want to change things constantly in this area. Investments do require patience. However, you should look at it within your net worth number and if you see a steady decline after a few months, I would meet with your advisor to see if changes need to be made.

- **Banking** – This is another area where you don't want to change constantly, but every year I would make sure I am getting the most for my money. Shop around and see what other local banks and credit unions are paying and move your accounts if necessary.

The key to these financial checkups is to keep a close eye on your finances and to make sure you are getting the best for your money. I have what I call a legacy book. This is a notebook with folders that has everything possible in it – insurance, banking, bills, assets, wills, etc. – anything that someone might need when I depart. I highly recommend you putting together one of these as a gift for your loved ones when the time comes. In doing so, you will be leaving them a true legacy and not a burden. I look at this book every three months to make sure every item is updated. This is a not only a great gift for your family, but a great guideline for your financial checkups.

If you want healthy teeth, you get a checkup every six months. If you want a healthy body, you get a checkup every year. And if you want healthy finances, you must perform financial checkups. Some items require a monthly checkup and some only a yearly one. The key is making sure you perform them for great health. These checkups are free, but they can cost you money if not performed as needed. Know where you stand, get the best for your money, and keep your finances as healthy as they can possibly be. Live long and prosper.

Debit Cards – Good and Bad

"I have a simple question – what are the advantages to using a debit card over a credit card? Are there any differences? Don't credit cards cover your purchases when debit cards don't?"

People who were around when debit cards first came out always struggle with these questions. In 1990, debit cards were in full swing and were quickly replacing the simple ATM card which only allowed you to get money out of your account through an ATM machine. With the debit card, you were able to use the credit system through your checking account. This allowed you to pay with a card even if you didn't have a credit card. This was also an opportunity for people without credit cards to start purchasing airline tickets, hotel rooms, rental cars, etc., which before could only be done with a credit card.

However, in the beginning, since this concept was new, many companies wouldn't accept "debit" cards even with the Visa or MasterCard logo because they knew it was tied to your checking account. There was nothing to protect them from non payment. This is not true today; however, many people still think the same as they did in the 1990's.

Today, you can do everything with a debit card that you can do with a credit card. You can travel, you can rent cars – you can literally do the exact same things, now with the same protection as a credit card from Visa and MasterCard directly. You no longer can say "I need a credit card" because this simply is not the case.

When it comes to making purchases, there are many advantages to using a debit card.

- The money comes directly out of your checking account.

- You are paying with cash you have, not cash you hope to one day have.

- There is no risk of spending more than you have.

- You are protected on all purchases made through the credit card system.

Credit cards are a risk. Because you are borrowing money, even for just a few days, there is always a chance things won't work out the way you intended. And if they don't, you end up paying way more for something than you would with a debit card. When you swipe your debit card, the money is taken immediately from your account with no risk.

I always recommend cash first and foremost because, as we talked about in the beginning, when swiping, we have a tendency to spend more than we mean to. With cash, you can only spend what you have. But if you are going to use a card, and there are many instances where you need to, I would always use a debit card over a credit card. You get all the benefits of a credit card without the risks. Life comes with enough risks – don't add one more to the mix.

Giving is Better Than Receiving

"Where does giving come into the money conversation? How much should we give?"

Giving is a heart issue – plain and simple. If you keep every dollar you have for yourself, you are being selfish with the blessings you have received. I know you may be thinking "It's my money – I earned it" and that's true, but it is always better to give than to receive.

This is a concept that is hard to teach. It is hard to explain how wonderful it is when you can help someone who is worse off than you – and there is always someone. The only thing I can say is I have done both and giving gives me a joy beyond words. Really the only thing I can say is try it.

There is no formula for giving. If you are a Christian, you may have been taught to give 10% to your local church. I believe, as a person of faith, that we need to give from our hearts not a formula. When you do this, you will give way beyond 10%. I have seen too many Christians give only 10% (to the penny) and that's it. They do it out of what they think is an obligation. There is no joy in that. But if you throw away the formula and give from the heart, you will end up giving more than 10%.

When I was getting out of debt, my giving was very limited. I gave occasionally to a cause that I felt strongly about and I tried to support the ministries that were encouraging and teaching me. You may be in this situation right now. You think you have nothing to give because you are barely staying afloat yourself. That's okay. Give what you can. And giving isn't just money – it can be time, it can be lending an ear, it can be giving someone a ride. Don't box giving into a money formula – begin to have a giving heart and the rest will follow.

You do need to give. We had a lady in our community who was an Uber driver to pay the bills. She didn't have a lot of money to give, but she gave rides to the homeless during the winter to the various shelters around. She gave what she could at the time. A person like that, when they begin to get out of debt and build wealth, will give like crazy. They won't limit themselves to just 10%.

I always teach give 10%, save 10%, and spend 80% as a guideline because you need somewhere to start. But please do not limit yourself to the 10%. And don't be ashamed if you can't do 10% right now. Again, giving is a heart issue. Work on getting your heart in the right place and the rest will work itself out.

Epilogue

I really hope that you enjoyed the book and found lots of hope and knowledge in its pages. When I was sitting on my living room floor 19 years ago, I had no idea how to tackle my $200,000 worth of debt, how to make more than $10,000 a year or even if I could. I had no clue where to start.

The goal of this book (and all of my books) and my life is to make sure that no one ever feels the way I felt. My mission is to serve you anyway that I can in a personal way. I always promised God that no matter how well known I became, I would never become unapproachable. I am by no means famous, but I want to always keep this promise.

If you ever have a question, email me. If you ever need someone to listen, email me. I want you to always have someone who cares and who wants nothing more than to see you succeed – not only in your finances, but in your life. You are never alone. There is always hope. If I can do it based on my numbers, reality, and knowledge, so can you.

I want to help anyway that I can and provide as many resources as possible. I have been where you are and I know that the last thing you think you can do when you are living paycheck to paycheck and believe you are broke is afford a personal finance coach. I understand that $100-150 a month just adds to the problem. It is worth every penny, but I wanted to create something that everyone could afford and still receive the personalized coaching you need.

Therefore, I developed the "50 Shades of Money Society". It is a special group of people who, for a very small monthly fee, will receive personalized coaching from me. There are three different plans that you can choose from based on your financial situation and of course, you can upgrade as your situation improves. It just breaks my heart to think someone couldn't improve their finances because they thought it was impossible or too expensive.

You took the first step in reading this book. Now take the next step and let's work together to make your finances the best they can be. Your financial future isn't based on your past or which side of the tracks you were born on. It is based on your decisions, your sacrifice and your belief that you can reach all of your goals over time.

Join our new society – you won't regret it!

Visit **www.debbiking.com** and click on the "Work With Me" tab to join today!